WHEN MOTHERS WORK, WHO PAYS?

WHEN MOTHERS WORK, WHO PAYS?

Martha Hahn Sugar

BERGIN & GARVEY
Westport, Connecticut • London

Library of Congress Cataloging-in-Publication Data

Sugar, Martha Hahn.
    When mothers work, who pays? / Martha Hahn Sugar.
      p. cm.
    Includes bibliographical references and index.
    ISBN 0–89789–383–2
    1. Working mothers—United States—Attitudes.   2. Children of
working mothers—United States—Attitudes. 3. Children of working
parents—United States—Attitudes. 4. Women—Employment—Public
opinion. 5. Public opinion—United States. I. Title.
HQ759.48.S84   1994
331.4′4′0973—dc20   93–43727

British Library Cataloguing in Publication Data is available.

Library of Congress Catalog Card Number: 93–43727
ISBN: 0–89789–383–2

First published in 1994

Bergin & Garvey, 88 Post Road West, Westport, CT 06881
An imprint of Greenwood Publishing Group, Inc.

Printed in the United States of America

The paper used in this book complies with the
Permanent Paper Standard issued by the National
Information Standards Organization (Z39.48–1984).

10 9 8 7 6 5 4 3 2 1

Contents

Figures and Tables

TABLES

WHEN MOTHERS WORK, WHO PAYS?

Introduction

Once my two daughters had outgrown diapers and entered pre-school, I felt convinced that I should get a job. Because the girls were out of the home several hours a day, they did not seem to need me as much as they did when they were toddlers. Without the constant labor involved in caring for infants, I began to feel guilty and bored staying at home. Periodically I cobbled together my resumé, answered newspaper advertisements and went on job interviews only to decide the position was too menial, dead-end, or distant from home. This scenario was repeated so often that I tried to figure out why I was reluctant to get out of the house and become employed. My children were getting older. They didn't really need me. My husband was supportive of my desire to work. We could certainly use the money. Still I held back from starting a career. Instead, I went to school for a Ph.D. in Marriage and Family Counseling, as much for the chance to stay in the home as for the opportunity for more education.

Following years of course work, the time had finally come to choose a topic for the dissertation. By that point, I had convinced myself that my reluctance to seek employment stemmed from the fact that my mother had stayed in the home during my childhood.

My reasoning was "I must not feel capable of combining family and employment because I had never witnessed my mother doing so." This seemed logical because so many women in my neighborhood were working full-time and rearing children while I sat, isolated, at home. On any given weekday, while walking around the block, my path crossed house after empty house where the mother worked outside the home and the children were in daycare, at the sitter's, or in school. Why was I so reluctant to go to work?

When my academic adviser suggested a dissertation on mothers and daughters, I jumped at the chance. It seemed the perfect opportunity to find out whether the presence of a home-mother or daily absence of a working mother during her daughter's youth and adolescence altered how her adult daughter perceived employment and parenting. In excitement, I planned the details with my advisers (who eyed me with pity as I mused about how to afford the needed tests and questionnaires if too many subjects volunteered for the study). Although obtaining sufficient numbers of subjects is usually a major problem for researchers, I assured my advisers that mothers aged twenty-five to forty-five would want to do *this* study. Even so, they cautioned me about the difficulty of finding enough subjects reared in intact homes or who had mothers with an exclusive housewife career. Luckily, they decided to let me stand or fall on my own; after two major local newspapers placed my request for subjects into articles, there were over 400 volunteers.

In just one day, my mother took 200 calls from women who wanted to participate. The volunteers told Mom how worried they were about the state of the American family, about how their working affected their children, and how happy they were to help. Some women volunteered by writing to an address at the university; they wrote their requests to take part and even added thank you notes to me for choosing the topic of motherhood and employment. The women were lawyers, nurses, professors, physicians, teachers, etc. Over 78% of the subjects described themselves as either professional or managerial.

The articles in the newspapers requested the participation of mothers between the ages of twenty-five and forty-five who had been reared in intact homes. I identified the research itself as a study dealing with attitudes about mothers, parenting, and employment. None of the subjects were told that for this study on motherhood, *they* were the daughters. The subjects' *mothers'* employment history determined into which group their questionnaires would be placed:

1. Women whose mothers had been home-mothers from the subjects' birth till the age of eighteen were placed in the home-mothers' group.

2. The part-time employment group consisted of women whose mothers had been employed part-time and/or had full-time employment for less than nine years during the subjects' childhood years (birth to age eighteen).

3. The full-time group consisted of subjects who indicated full-time employment by the mother for at least nine years.

WHO WERE THE SUBJECTS?

Within three months, subjects returned 71% of the questionnaires, yielding usable tests from 253 subjects. Ninety subjects had been reared by home-mothers, 129 had part-time employed mothers, and 34 subjects had mothers who had worked full-time for a total of nine to eighteen years of the subjects' childhood. In the part-time group, some of the subjects' mothers had employment for as little as one year, part-time or full-time. When my advisers and I were developing the criteria for the subject selection, we used the rationale that the study would be more meaningful (impactful) if the subjects came from favorable (no parental divorce, generally middle class) backgrounds. Therefore, we did not attempt to mirror society as a whole. In this way we avoided the confounding variables of divorce, poverty, separation, etc. The resultant sample was fairly homogenous in its makeup. The subjects were generally married, professional, white women (representing combinations of twenty-five different ethnic identities) with a mean age of 36.7 years and averaged 2.22 children apiece. Geographically, the women resided primarily in urban and suburban areas located in northeastern Ohio. Although I suppose some will criticize the demographics of the study because it is not an exact reflection of America, my goal was to determine the effects of maternal employment or nonemployment. The homogeneity of the subjects only strengthens the apparent differences of the three groups that were based upon the subjects' mothers' employment status.

One difficulty in studying the resultant effects of maternal employment over a thirty-eight-year span (1947–1985) is that the demographics of the United States, as a whole, altered tremendously. For instance, in the year the oldest subjects were one-year-olds (1948), 26% of mothers with children under the age of eighteen were employed outside the home. Although that is a substantial percentage, it is quite different from the 62.1% rate of maternal employment by the time the youngest subjects were turning eighteen in 1985. By very rough averaging, approximately 44% of mothers were employed (part-time or full-time) from 1948 to 1985. In comparison, more of the subjects' mothers in the Sugar Study had been employed, at some time, while rearing the subjects (64%). The reason for the difference between those percentages is most likely that women who had employed mothers had greater interest in participating in a study regarding maternal employment.

An additional source of confusion in studying maternal employment involves the work histories of women with children. Mothers in the labor force have traditionally not had consistent work histories. Because of changing family needs, they may work full-time one year, part-time the next and not at all the third year. In the Sugar Study, the mother of each subject had a pattern of employment that was unlike the pattern of most other subjects' mothers. National demographics suggest that around 70% of employed mothers work full-time, leaving 30% working part-time during any given week. Of the subjects whose mothers had worked outside the home a similar ratio was noted. Sixty-four percent of the 163 subjects with working mothers had mothers who had worked full-time (at some time) during the subjects' childhood.

The care and attention the women gave in filling out the study materials made it obvious that the subject of motherhood and employment was one of great concern (almost 60% of the subjects had employment outside the home either part-time or full-time at the time of the study). Some subjects worked on their questionnaires over a period of days or weeks. One subject reported taking weeks to carefully complete her questionnaire. Subjects frequently answered the two essay questions at the end of the questionnaire with lengthy and thoughtful autobiographies or philosophies (over 200 typed pages after transcription). Others put their names and phone numbers on the anonymous questionnaires, offering to be interviewed in person. One subject whose response arrived very late wrote:

> Sorry this is so late being returned. Even if you can't use it in your survey, I wanted you to know how I felt about some of these issues. Thanks for listening. (*To this subject—yes, your questionnaire was used.*)

Little did I know, when starting this study, how much the findings would change my beliefs about mothering and the needs of daughters. After the questionnaires were tabulated and statistically analyzed, my advisers and I were surprised by and concerned with the results. Far from discovering that daughters of working mothers felt better about themselves and their careers because of their full-time working mother role models, we found the daughters significantly less happy about themselves in virtually every sphere. In an era marked by the increasing presence of mothers in the labor force, the results of the survey suggested serious consequences for a substantial percentage of daughters reared by employed women.

This book was written out of respect for the millions of women who are brave enough to rear children in an uncertain age and for the hundreds of mothers caring enough to volunteer their private opinions and thoughts to an unknown researcher. As I read through the 258 questionnaires, tears would frequently spring to my eyes. I had become a witness to the deepest pain and joy imaginable. The response of the subjects evoked feelings of responsibility in me to tell their story. Readers of this volume may not feel comfortable with either the statistical results of the study or the author's interpretations of the findings. This cannot be helped. I owe the women of the study the opportunity for their truth to be known. This book explores the issues of maternal employment, mothers, daughters, and how women perceive themselves and their society.

The arrangement of the following chapters provides a brief social context, history and research review for the phenomena of childhood and maternal employment in the United States. In addition, each chapter will contain encapsulated subject comments or autobiographies. Although most subjects wrote comments about their feelings, some women revealed especially touching glimpses of their lives with their mothers or children. Each subject response is labeled to tell the reader whether the subjects' mother had been a

home-mother "HM"

part-time employed mother "PM"

full-time employed mother "FM"

Next to the designation of maternal employment status is a number that indicates which question the subject had answered of the following two queries:

1. How did your mother's work, inside the home or outside the home, affect you?

2. How do you feel about your work, inside or outside the home, while raising children?

For example, if the designation under the response is PM2, it means that the subject's mother had worked outside the home part-time (according to the previous definition) during the subject's childhood and the question being answered was the second.

The content of this book involves the exploration of one puzzle piece: maternal employment. In no way does it explain or even attempt to understand the complex relationships involved between fathers, government, laws, education, or social services and the lives of children. Mothers are incalculably important to their sons and daughters, but we would be unfair and unrealistic to assume that only mothers are to blame if their children experience difficulty. Nor should we ignore the influence mothers do have on their offspring.

Throughout history, women have borne the burden of child rearing. Men have traditionally refused to help in the softer, and therefore less important, chore of parenting. Even today, in academics, the soft sciences (sociology, psychology, history) are often viewed distainfully by academicians in the hard sciences (math, physics, chemistry). Despite the current grass roots movement for men to become more involved with their children, the traditional father still seems to feel somewhat squeamish while changing the diapers of an infant, caressing a distraught child, or comforting a depressed adolescent. Yet we seldom suggest that such a man is a bad father. As long as the man is supporting his family financially and is physically present in the home, he is usually viewed with admiration by society. On the other side of the coin, women have been expected to provide for all the physical, intellectual and emotional needs of their children at the same time they worked outside the home to enhance or totally provide for the economic welfare of their families. If the children failed to develop as compassionate and responsible adults, the mother was usually blamed. What with Sigmund Freud's successful career of mother damning, even when children were flourishing, it was assumed to be in spite of rather than because of the mother's influence.

Far from being admired by society for their dedication to work and family, employed mothers frequently felt looked down upon by their extended families or community at large. Working women were viewed with suspicion. How could women produce quality children and give a quality performance in the workplace? Could it be that the male dominated power structure had expected and wanted women to fail? If so, women in the past two generations have proved their ability, drive and dedication to involve themselves in the economic lifeblood of our nation. But at what cost? At whose expense?

The research this book comprises was based on a correlational study. This means that statistically significant findings showed some relationship between maternal employment and the attitudes and circumstances subsequently reported by the subjects involved. A correlation between variables does not prove a cause and effect relationship. The statistical measures examined each of the maternal employment groups as a whole. Contrary to many of the subjects reared by employed mothers, some women in the full-time maternal employment group reported feeling satisfied with their lives, parenting and careers. Similarly, some women in the home-mother group reported feeling less competent as parents, dissatisfied with their lives and unhappy with their careers. The fact that someone's mother worked full-time during her childhood does not automatically mean she has suffered damage from her mother's employment. We cannot even state with absolute certainty that maternal employment or nonemployment was the reason for the striking differences found among the three groups. In the same way, *no one can say that maternal employment did not cause the differences.* The consistent patterns in the findings of the Sugar Study lend persuasive evidence to the suggestion that maternal employment played a major role in the development of depression, dissatisfaction, and an impaired sense of self-efficacy among the daughters of employed mothers.

For the better part of a year, I have been trying to find any reason why the findings were a mistake or an aberration. The findings simply appeared too consistent and too perfect. Every time a new computer report came out, I would still be suspicious, wondering where the flaws were. Only after returning to the original questionnaires and rereading the subject responses did I have to admit that the charts and graphs matched the comments made by the subjects themselves. I am personally convinced that the findings of the Sugar Study reflected differences in the attitudes and opinions of women who had been reared by home-mothers and women whose mothers had worked full-time or part-time. However, you the reader, must examine the results for yourself.

Perhaps the time has arrived to take an honest look at some of the consequences of a common parenting dilemma: Should mothers work outside the home while rearing children?

1

The American Family, What's Happening to Us?

Seldom does a day pass without the publication of at least one article or book lamenting the disintegration of the American family. Newspapers spew out article after article about elementary school children who take weapons to class, and teenagers with nothing better to do than kill (anyone) as the pastime of the 1990s. Children are angrier, more frustrated, and depressed more frequently, at a younger age, than ever before. Some researchers blame teenage pregnancy, unwed motherhood, divorce, and television for the increase of drug use, violence, crime and depression among youths. Other writers indict the era of permissiveness generated by the sixties, self-absorbed baby boomers and a "me first" attitude that has eroded the concepts of family loyalty, enjoyment of work, and altruism. Whatever the causes for the seeming decline in moral and social values, without solutions and the people with the will to implement them, the values of life in the United States are destined to deteriorate.

Perhaps most unsettling of all is the rapidity with which our society changed; those of us born between 1945 and 1965 remember how Mother kept a clean house and made a welcoming home. Father worked during the day and came home predictably at 5:30 p.m.; he found a tidy home, happy children and dinner on the table. We knew that everything was just the way it was supposed to be. Even if our family did not match the ideal, we knew that everyone else's mother greeted her at the door after a hard day of school or play with warm chocolate chip cookies, cold milk and a loving hug.

My mother mostly always worked and while my other friends went home to a "stay-at-home" mother and had home-made cookies waiting for them, I went home to an empty house after school. I swore I wouldn't do that to my children. That's why I stay at home with them. (FM1)

I never liked it. I felt cheated. The other kids seemed to have more of the "normal" family life. Chocolate chip cookies & milk after school—things like that. (FM1)

The postwar baby-boom epoch was, perhaps, one of the unique periods of family history. Because the United States enjoyed a virtual monopoly in the devastated world economy, the standard of living improved tremendously, permitting unprecedented numbers of Americans to escape from poverty. Never before had so many families been permitted the luxury of a middle-class life-style. The financial security garnered by the parents was passed on to the children in the form of improved health care, more education, and material assets. In addition, the majority of children enjoyed the full-time presence of a caring adult because the social mores of the 1950s included an expectation for the mother to remain in the home.

My mother stayed home to raise 7 children—that was a vocation. Now that the children are married, my mother works as a receptionist in my father's office. It was great having the secure feeling of having a parent at home–to listen, to care for, to share with us and guide us. I am glad I am able to stay at home to raise our children—there's much to be said for the parent "being there" for their children. (HM1)

Having my mother home gave me a great sense of stability and security. I highly respected her intelligence, creativity, and devotion to my father and us. She not only gave us her availability, but was a great source of wisdom. (HM1)

It gave me security to have my mother at home. She was there
when I needed her and it was a wonderful heritage for me to
pass on to my children. I am grateful to my mother. (*HM1*)

American society of the fifties assumed better psychological adjustment for children reared in intact homes, with a mother present,
because the homes were thought more stable and predictable.
Neighbors looked upon children whose mothers worked with pity.
In some instances the mother *had* to enter the labor pool because
of widowhood, divorce or insufficient finances. However, she generally went to work feeling guilty. The employed mothers often
experienced remorse at leaving their children in the hands of others.
They frequently believed that work and home both suffered from
neglect as they straddled two worlds.

Most of my friends' mothers were full-time homemakers and
we felt sorry for the few friends we had whose mothers were
employed outside the home and when parents were unable
to attend school functions or who went home to empty houses
after school. (*PM1*)

For women who became adults from the 1940s through most of
the 1960s, the dominant culture predetermined clearly defined sex
roles: women were supposed to marry and have children, in that
order. If a young woman went to college, it was often with her
parents' implicit expectation that she would come home with a husband. The college degree itself was merely an added bonus. With
her marriage and the birth of children, society expected the woman
to assume most of the emotional, social, and physical responsibility
for her family. In return, she was supposed to be "cared for" by her
more dynamic and dominant husband. In actuality, the experience
of the "cared for" wife led to a tendency to keep the woman childlike
and dependent. With gender expectations and stereotypes of pas-
sivity and dependence widely accepted, researchers began to recognize negative consequences for housewives. The mother and wife
who was not permitted to mature emotionally or intellectually because of her subservient role as "the little woman" was diagnosed
more often with depression and impaired self-esteem.

Television reruns, the scrapbook of the twentieth century, portrayed idyllic families in the 1950s and early 1960s with "Father Knows Best," "Ozzie and Harriet," and "Leave It to Beaver." In a 1960 article for *Good Housekeeping* magazine (Overstreet, H. & Overstreet, B., pg. 183), the following was written regarding the need for women to remain in the home:

> Women are tough-fibered. They can stand a lot when they are sustained by the fact that love is their reason: love of a child, a husband, a friend–love of the fumbling human race, of life itself. What they cannot stand is a prolonged abdication of the nurturing role. They become brittle—breakable—if the life-supporting enterprises of friendship and neighboring are subordinated to social and economic competition. They tear themselves to pieces when they say to a child or a husband who has something to tell them, "Don't bother me now. Can't you see I'm busy?"

Even as the Overstreets wrote that article, more than one of four married women, with children under the age of eighteen, were in paid employment outside the home. The ideal family situation of the fifties was already slipping away.

A rising divorce rate during the sixties led women to realize that they could no longer rely upon the security of marriage for their entire lives. Indeed, with the advent of no-fault divorce, many women, having given decades of their lives to husbands and children, found themselves abandoned, middle-aged, and with no experience or marketable skills. Those women faced emotional devastation by their husbands and financial devastation by the legal system. In essence, the women had been cheated by the very husbands and society they had believed in and worked so hard to support. Realizing their precarious position, women began to protect themselves by hardening their idealistic views of men and the established order. They also started fostering, in daughters, the belief in education, work skills, and an expectation to combine parenting and career as essential survival skills.

As a result of social forces such as women's liberation and expanded perceptions of choice in life-styles and occupations in the 1960s, many women demanded a larger definition of their cultural role. They challenged existing sexual stereotypes. Concomitantly changes in the culture, brought on by the burgeoning baby-boom generation then reaching maturity, forced everyone (men and women alike) to change the way they saw their world.

I always felt that my mother was a very intelligent, attractive and capable woman who could have done anything she put her mind to. Although her background (immigrant parents who did not see post high school education as a valuable thing for a woman) and the era in which I grew up (the 50's) did not really give her many choices, she never felt that working in the home and raising children full time was a job with little value. . . . She was a wonderful homemaker and a good mother who appeared to thoroughly enjoy her job. She always said she had plenty of time to work for pay when we girls were grown. And she did. She recently retired at 65 after 22 years in a non-traditional field and has the distinction of being the first woman (and only woman so far) to be promoted to a management position. She was extremely supportive of me when I made the choice to leave my career after the birth of my first son and became a full-time homemaker and mother. (PM1)

Heightened social awareness of those decades (1960s and 1970s) made us realize that the stereotype of "family" in the previous generation was inadequate for vast numbers of Americans. With the divorce rate rising and an increase of out-of-wedlock births, "family" was frequently a mother and her children or blended families created from two previous marriages. In response, a more humane attitude was born to prevent the stigma allotted to the children of such families. We began to understand that the "bastard" child had no guilt in his or her own conception; that the children of divorce should not be punished or shunned because of the decision of their parents. Unfortunately, the reasonable and compassionate attitude of accepting alternative life-styles (for the sake of the innocent) became translated by some individuals into permission to ignore social conventions altogether. Cohabitation became sensible instead of shocking. Divorce became a right rather than a tragedy. The rallying cries: Freedom from Sexual repression! Freedom from marriage! Freedom from responsibility! altered the perceptions and actions of a generation. We have begun to discover the price of our freedoms.

While stereotypically saccharine families mirrored the postwar generation of parents (if only in desire), the dysfunctional families depicted by *Married with Children, Roseanne,* and *The Simpsons* displayed our fears for families in the 1990s. Most of us have recognized our society has taken a wrong turn. In the last thirty years, we have witnessed what appeared to be the subversion of all the rules and regulations we thought held society together. Criminals seem to have more civil rights than victims. Murderers walk out of prison early, only to kill again, because of simple mistakes made on arrest warrants or overcrowding in the prisons. Burglars sue the homeowners who shot them out of fear and in self-defense, and win. Because of this, our values of honesty, truthfulness, altruism, and belief in the work ethic have weakened. Even the most law-abiding citizens begin to question their rationale for remaining civilized when society appears to reward disobedience, as indicated in the following letter to the editor (*Akron Beacon Journal,* April 29, 1993, p. A18):

> Why are such benefits awarded these criminals? . . . Don't think for a minute that our children don't pick up on these insulting differences: "Yeah, Jimmy, let's steal a million. We won't even go to jail."
>
> Such judicial/social imbalances reflect an overall change in our business, social and family values.
>
> Crime is crime, and white-collar crime, such as the alleged bingo swindle is more deplorable as it is a violation of public trust by two already well-to-do individuals. It not only insults our sense of equal justice, judicial effectiveness, crime deterrence and our government and economic system, but indeed, our society's moral fiber.
>
> Steven S. Canton

No social organization was left untouched by the changes in public perception. The idea of subordinating one's own needs for the sake of others seemed neurotic, sick or somehow deficient. Instead, financial profit and loss became the moral measuring stick for a generation. Even the sacrifices made in the name of motherhood drew attack from groups that equated maternal altruism with martyrdom. For many women, the freedom of choice to work outside the home for pay became a twisted mandate to have careers whether they wanted to or not. Even so, some women balked at leaving their homes and children. Unfortunately, mothers who decided to follow the traditional model of motherhood had little support or respect from society. At best, mothers who chose to remain in the home to care for their own children were often made to appear selfish as they "wasted" their education performing (seemingly) menial tasks. At worst, stay-at-home mothers were viewed as dimwitted leeches, considered by their working peers as unable or unwilling to help support their families financially.

> Though I sometimes worry that I'm "wasting" my teaching skills and academic ability, I am convinced that no one needs me more than my girls, and that no one can take my place in their lives. (*PM2*)

> Sometimes I feel I have not achieved as much as I desire in my career. I would like to further my education. I feel guilty about these feelings. I feel that I need to "sacrifice" my educational aspirations to raise my family. (That must have been "taught.") But I have not "given up" on those desires and one day I will further my educational goals. (*PM2*)

> I graduated from one of the best schools in the country (M.I.T.) and know professionally I could have "gone much further" had I chosen to. However incomprehensible my choices may seem to some, I am very comfortable with them. (*HM2*)

In spite of those negative attitudes, many mothers who remained in the home saw the opportunity to rear their own children as a luxury. They firmly believed that they were the best care givers for their children and that in that capacity, they provided an invaluable service to society. With mothers in the workplace out numbering home-mothers two to one, books such as *Home by Choice* and *What's a Smart Woman Like You Doing at Home?* were shocking and revolutionary because they gave permission for mothers to rear their own children.

I enjoy being home with my 2 kids! Some days are better than others . . . like any job. Some days I feel I wish I could work outside the home, eat lunch out, have adults to talk to, dress nicely, punch out when the day is done, but I always think . is it worth it? Many of my friends work outside and have their kids in day care. Most of the time they complain how their child is sick, or everyone is rushed, how hectic things are, or they justify the choice they've made . . . "Oh the day care center is so wonderful they love it there." or "Our sitter is great . . . she writes down in a notebook all the things they have done that day." Almost all of our friends who are expecting their first child, the woman is planning on working at least 4 days. They think about sitters & nannies from the start. Most "have to" work to pay for expensive homes, cars, country clubs, fashionable clothes, & vacations. Sometimes I feel like a total outsider choosing to stay at home, I also have chosen to breast feed my kids. Most of these friends think that breast feeding is totally gross and that you should only do it for about 1 month (I've nursed my son till 9 months, hopefully I'll do the same for my new daughter. I feel I have made a choice to put my children first). I enjoy being with them, I feel that is my work—it means sacrifice sometimes, but it's worth it to be there for my kids. Yes sometimes I get frustrated but who doesn't! I love my children and feel they need me home. I wish others (my peers) could understand. (*HM2*)

You only have one chance to raise children, that is why I chose to stay home with my children. (*PM2*)

I feel a deep responsibility to my children and that means staying home to care for their needs. It is a blessing for me to be able to stay home full time and I would do that even if we had to sacrifice financially. I like staying home and managing the house and feel that I am good at it. The hard part is the demands on my time from my two young children. Also, being a homemaker can be lonely. (*PM2*)

I feel staying home with my children is the most important job I could do. There are times when I need other intellectual

activities. Being home does not challenge my intellect a great
deal. (PM2)

As women, we were taught that we could *have it all*: the career,
family, personal goals, and material possessions. On the surface,
perhaps we did. The workplace offered us adult companionship,
verbal reinforcement for a job well done, and monetary compen-
sation. In comparison to the world of employment, housework and
mothering were dull and unrewarding with their repetitive, un-
ending labor and nonexistent praise. Small wonder mothers entered
the world of work in unprecedented numbers.

> I needed more than kids & T.V., but not enough to ever miss
> out on any family activities—I never miss a ball game or event
> they are in. Home & family always come first. I think I man-
> aged both job & kids well. They know I want them & love
> them all. (PM2)

> There's always too much to do + not enough time! Definitely
> not enough time to just play with my children. It's frustrating
> + aggravating + sometimes depressing. (PM2)

> I am grateful for the lifestyle which we have, but sometimes
> wish things could be simpler. Although the whole point of the
> women's movement in the 60's and 70's was designed to give
> freedom of choice to women, I think what it really did was
> make things MORE limiting. It doesn't seem acceptable any-
> more to just have a job or to just be a mother. It seems that
> all the magazine articles about successful women describe
> women who have responsible jobs, successful marriages, fab-
> ulous children and who look gorgeous! These are the role
> models of today's woman?! My point is that society still expects
> women to do most of the child-rearing and household chores
> AS WELL AS hold down a job and look great; in other words,
> be a super-woman! Oh, for the good old days! (PM2)

Employed mothers interpreted themselves and their lives differ-
ently than mothers who remained in the home. Many of them were
no longer dependent upon their husbands for their material welfare.
They had personal identities independent of their husband's position

in the community. Employed women had a source of self-esteem in their own careers. The money women contributed to the family evolved from a mere supplement to equal their husband's income. Their paychecks became as essential to the family's material standing as their husband's.

[*Author's note*: Could the case be made that the increasing ability women developed to be financially independent may have given inadequate or borderline husbands the spurious justification they needed to abandon their own responsibilities toward wives and children?]

> The most important thing for me growing up was that Mom was always there when I came home from school. She was a teacher and substituted when I was in grade school and high school. She also did some tutoring in the home. I was quite proud that she was intelligent. Sometimes she took us all out for dinner with "her money." She managed the household very well. (*PM1*)

> It made me proud of her when she worked outside the home. I learned to do many household tasks to help her and she always showed appreciation and praise to me for it. I think she was more satisfied with working outside the home because it made her more financially independent. (*PM1*)

Despite the sociological and economical imperatives for women to work outside the home, the political and social structure in the United States failed to respond to the needs of dual-income families. Little was done by government or industry to provide quality child care. Even when such care was available, it was too costly for the majority of families and failed to take into account special needs of ill or handicapped children. Mothers constantly found themselves in an impossible bind: trying to manage unpredictable family situations within rigidly defined and artificial structures of the industrial world. How could mothers hope to maintain personal integrity while choosing between emergency child care needs and the incessant demands of the workplace? How many women have lied to employers and used up their own sick days to stay home with an ailing child?

> I have felt anxious in the past (when my son was very ill) and I am enjoying the lifting of the burden of health difficulties

(he is enjoying very good health at this time). It is extremely difficult to deal with caring for a sick child when the worry of losing a job exists. (PM2)

Due to financial problems and many moves because of my husband's job, I felt I had to work. Of course, I also had to juggle home and work. I was usually, if not always exhausted, because of the pace I had to keep. I received no help from my husband around the house or raising our children. When I decided to go back to college at age 35, I had to quit after one year because I was physically and mentally unable to work, take care of a house & children and meet the demands of college. (PM2)

[Author's note: While it is true that some fathers are increasingly accepting the responsibility to help out in such emergencies, their assistance is usually just that, helping out. While mothers average ninety minutes per day with their children, fathers spend just seventeen minutes with their children daily (C. Zick, "Moms Can Have Kids, Work too," Akron Beacon Journal, pp. A1 and A12, April 28, 1993). The burden of child-rearing dilemmas (as well as household tasks) generally remains the mother's domain.]

Social support for working mothers turned out to be empty permission, without supplying the essential nuts and bolts for integrating family and employment: quality child care, sick child care, maternity leave, flexible work schedules, housekeeping relief, etc. The overwhelming attitude of "society" was that women may perform the work of men as long as they also perform women's work. When the eight hour workday ended, wives and mothers returned home to an additional stint of housework, child care, and meal preparation. To worsen matters, because women had complained so loudly and fought so hard for greater equity between the sexes such as equal pay for equal work, mothers then perceived they had little room for protest.

To deal with the guilt of leaving their children and especially for enjoying their careers, women convinced themselves they had no choice financially except to work. At the same time, they bought in to the philosophy that happy parents created happy children. Mothers believed that their choices to divorce, remarry, obtain material possessions and build careers that made them feel more fulfilled and in control would trickle down to create happy children. At the minimum, mothers believed children would not be hurt by their parents' life-style choices. Mothers were told by professionals that the *quality* of time with their children was what counted, rather than the *quantity* of time. In fact, many experts in child rearing espoused the philosophy that children did as well or as poorly regardless of who performed the child care. In essence, mothers were considered by some scholars to have little or no impact on the adult outcomes of their children. In reviewing recent maternal employment research, the authors of *Megatrends for Women* reassured mothers that absence due to employment did not hurt, and was even good for, children. If one was to believe the experts, mothers had become obsolete.

> I love my work and feel I'm a much better parent with it because I have too much energy as it is. My daughter would be up a creek if all that energy were directed to her. As it is I probably have done more and made life too easy so work for me is my sanity check. (*FM2*)

> I work part time primarily to get out of the house to be with the "outside" world. The twins are usually home with Daddy on days or evenings I work. The time I spend with my kids I'm all theirs. The time I get for myself (just to get out and feel productive in the real world) makes me a better mommy. (*FM2*)

> I enjoy my time outside of the home, stimulation of my job, but it seems like I never get caught up, never get everything done at home. I think I'm a better parent after getting away from my children at work for a while. I appreciate better the time I have to spend with them. (*FM2*)

When teenage drug use, depression, suicide, violence and crimes by children steadily increased over the past few decades, we looked on in confusion. Mavens of the culture believed the source of the problem was rooted in the schools, economic recessions, a changing social context or a plethora of other issues. Teachers blamed the inattentiveness of parents and fiscal insolvency. Parents threw up

their hands in despair, assuring anyone who would listen that problems were caused by everyone else's kids, lax school discipline, the
prevalence of drugs, or society at large. Like a dog chasing its own
tail, we each thought we couldn't possibly be the reason for our
children's unhappiness and unruliness, because we were doing just
fine. We were doing what we had been socialized to do by psychologists, sociologists, teachers, and especially the media. We had
it all!

The problem is, our children didn't seem to be getting "it" at all.
They were getting lost in the shuffle between the demands of their
working parents and the demands by society to grow up—fast.

I think that if we can afford for me to stay home—I should.
It is so difficult being with a baby all day and I'm the baby's
mom. I just don't think any other person could care as much
as I do for the welfare of my child. Sure, sometimes I miss
being part of the working world—but I've got lots of years
ahead to get back to a career. Children are so formative in the
early years and I want to do everything I can to form a caring,
loving decent human being. Maybe I'll succeed, maybe I won't
but at least I'll know I tried. I think as a society we are at a
breaking point. Either we start really caring about our kids
again or there's no turning back—the downward slide will
continue. I think a lot of kids today don't know limits and have
no manners. I want to teach my children to respect others and
to have good manners and to always concern themselves with
the well being of all people. I may be living in dream world—
but it's a dream worthy of pursuing. Like I said earlier in 5–
10 years I'll be able to rejoin the workforce. But why work
outside the house now if I don't need to financially? I can
accomplish so much at home. (*PM2*)

I am one of eleven children. I have five younger siblings. The
most pronounced effect of my mother's returning to work was
that I was given a lot of responsibility for my siblings (I was
sixteen, they were 4–14). I felt abandoned. More strongly, I
felt that they'd been abandoned. I felt over-burdened. I
learned responsibility and developed a deep parental love for
them because of the experience. I felt quite experienced as a

parent before my oldest daughter was born—I often mistakenly call her by my little sister's name. On the other side, I felt proud of my mother for her accomplishment in finishing school. I still tell the story with pride for her determination and hard work. (PM1)

My mother worked to put my father through college after he got out of the service. She went to work when I was about 14 months old and worked outside the home until I was 4 1/2 when my brother was born. I spent the mornings at my paternal grandmother's house and in the afternoons, I was cared for by my maternal grandmother.

Being the first grandchild on both sides, I was indulged and spoiled. Each grandmother did her housework when I wasn't there, so she devoted a tremendous amount of attention on me. As a result, I was read to and played with several hours a day. I think this contributed to my high IQ and my academic success.

The drawback was that there were no children for me to play with. Consequently, my maternal grandmother took me to Sunday School every Sunday. She had to sit with me in class because, even at age 3, I had an extreme fear of abandonment which has haunted me my entire life. I do not know if this fear was related to my mother's employment.

When I was 4 1/2 my brother was born and mom stayed home. Six months later I began kindergarten and my fear of abandonment became extreme. Since kindergarten was half/day, I made it through, but my Grandpa mostly picked me up from school.

In first grade, I had a "breakdown." I refused to go to school and fought and bit and kicked and screamed and put every ounce of my energy into not going. Finally mom took me to a psychologist who said I was worried about mom and (the baby) at home. Looking back on the situation, I remember having horrible nightmares that I came home from school and my house was empty and my family had moved without me. Again, I'm not sure if this was a result of my mother's employment or the extreme "threat" a sibling posed to a spoiled little girl.

On the positive side, because of my mother working when I was little (and part time when I was a teen) I never even considered being a stay at home mom, except when my kids were infants and toddlers. At least that was our plan when we married, but the economy forced us into other plans. (*PM1*)

2

What Does It Mean to Be a Child?

CHILDHOOD RECONSIDERED

The concept of childhood is a relatively modern invention. Historians suggest that the "traditional" concept of childhood, beginning at birth and extending to eighteen, did not become widely accepted until the twentieth century. For much of U.S. history the idea that children were to be protected and nurtured beyond infancy was considered wasteful and injurious to the child.

In colonial times, the high death rate among infants precluded sentimental attachment between parent and child: even if the infant survived, the philosophy of that age taught parents that children were born evil and needed to have sin rooted out of them. Spare the rod and spoil the child meant that unbeaten children became spoiled; our ancestors would have been appalled by the permissive attitude that became prevalent in the 1960s that physical punishment itself damaged the children. In colonial America and in the early years after the birth of the United States, labor was expected from children not only because of the harsh conditions of existence but because parents believed that "idle hands do the devil's work."

Children usually worked next to their parents in the field and in the home. Fathers taught their sons to farm and care for the animals while daughters learned homemaking skills at their mother's knee. As was common in Europe, boys and girls as young as seven were often apprenticed to tradesmen or other households to learn a living and ease the financial burden of the family. Unlike in Europe, where the infants of the poor were often sent away to "baby farms" to enable the impoverished mother to work, in America infants usually remained with their mothers. The first studies regarding maternal employment investigated the high mortality rate among the infants of working mothers in Europe early in the nineteenth century. One must speculate whether the interest in the babies' welfare was initiated out of humane concern for the infants or materialistic concern about the source of future workers.

As the industrial revolution of the early 1800s provided paid employment outside the home, owners and managers of factories and textile mills viewed women as cheap and dexterous labor. Women, previously occupied as wives and mothers, earned extra cash income that often made the difference between subsistence living standards and relative comfort for their families. American women typically relied upon older children, or extended family, to care for their young children while they worked. These arrangements were not always possible, however. Out of necessity, some working mothers took their children with them to the workplace. In fact, the children of women laborers would frequently be used as workers and paid minimally for their labor. Children as young as four could be found laboring in textile mills alongside their older sisters and brothers. In southern mills, a full 30% of the employees were children. Boys accounted for 20% of coal miners in the late eighteen hundreds. Legislation paving the way for the abolition of child labor in the United States was not passed until 1912.

The Victorian era of the late nineteenth century provided the stimulus for a new concept of society. Childhood gained recognition as a unique period in an individual's life. However, children were reared as entities separate from their parents' social and commercial ventures. Children were frequently treated with aloofness if not coldness. Child care experts of the day urged parents to keep their children on strict schedules. If infants cried between scheduled feedings, they were supposed to be ignored, or else their moral fiber would be destroyed. Parents were admonished not to hug, kiss or otherwise coddle their children.

Just as the Victorian age altered the viewpoint of society toward children, expectations for women changed. Men and women were to be segregated by gender, into specific spheres of influence in which men were to perform their duties actively in public while women were supposed to be the domestic guardians of religious and ethical values. This meant that women, in general, and mothers specifically were to stay at home, out of the commercial world of men. In 1890, only 5% of married women were employed; however, the actual number of married mothers with young children in the work force was certainly much lower as suggested by Hoffman and Nye (1974, p. 3).

In 1940, the U.S. Department of Labor estimated that 8.6% of married women with children under the age of seventeen were in the labor force. The number of mothers who worked outside the home steadily increased for the next five decades. In 1948, 26.0% of mothers with children under the age of eighteen worked outside the home. By 1991, 66.8% of married women with children under the age of eighteen were in the labor force; approximately three-quarters of those women worked full-time.

Despite the increase in maternal participation in the work force, societal acceptance and institutional assistance failed to keep pace with the changing needs of the American family. Families used many strategies to accommodate their child care requirements: organized day care center, in-home baby sitter, care giver's home, care by a relative, or company provided child care near a parent's employment. Mothers of school age children may have arranged for before/after school activities or supervision by a neighbor or may have decided the child was capable enough to stay home alone.

[*Author's note*: In my own experience, I witnessed some families caring for the older child (aged 10–14) by providing a house key around the neck and a bag of candy to keep them quiet. Other families "handled" the child care issue by having the child roam the neighborhood (locked out) until the parents arrived home, hours later.]

EARLY RESEARCH

Maternal employment was so unusual at the beginning of this century that it did not become much of a research topic in the

United States until a 1920 study conducted by Dr. Woodbury in Bedford, Massachusetts, who found a 40% higher death rate among the infants of employed mothers compared to the infants reared by mothers who stayed in the home (reported in Hughes, 1925). In the same year, the Philadelphia Board of Education issued a report that suggested maternal employment aggravated the higher than normal rates of retardation noted in the city schools. In the early part of the twentieth century, "retarded" was the word used to label a child whenever the grade level did not match the child's age; causes of this retardation included feeblemindedness, slow development, speaking English as a second language, and irregular school attendance. Members of the school board believed the children of working mothers fell below grade level in achievement because of the emotional burden of having an employed mother and the family's need to have the older children at home for child care, errands, or housekeeping. In addition, board members suggested that unsupervised children were more likely to be truant from school. Another study, conducted in Chicago in 1917, found similar results for the children of employed mothers. Social workers, concerned about the needs of the children of employed mothers, opened day nurseries to help ease the problem. Efforts were also made to teach parents about the need for their older children to remain in school.

> I was like a mother to my sister who is 7 1/2 yrs. younger than me. Had to start dinners and help with dishes. Had to help with their homework at times. *(PM1)*

> It made me grow up faster. I now had her responsibility of making supper, doing laundry and looking after my younger brothers. *(PM1)*

Both the necessity and incidence of mothers' working outside the home began to decrease after 1911. This happened, in part, because of the inception of widow's pensions that enabled widows with young children to stay home to rear their children. At the same time, social sentiment strongly encouraged women to stay in the home for the sake of their children. During the Great Depression of the 1930s, married women were often fired or not hired because of the commonly held belief that if a job were available it should be given to a man. Although in the early part of the twentieth century the Bureau of Labor did not keep records on the presence of mothers in the work force, a study by the Committee on Wage-Earning Mothers in 1918 and 1919 (Hoffman and Nye, 1974) found a maternal employment rate of approximately 14%. By 1940, the rate of maternal employment, in the United States, had fallen to less than 9%.

Women began again to enter the work force in substantial numbers after the United States entered World War II. Suddenly, the stiff sanctions against mothers' working outside the home were abandoned in the interest of fighting tyranny abroad. Between 1940 and 1948, work force participation of mothers with children under the age of eighteen had tripled to 26%. Research into the possible negative effects of maternal employment during the war was all but abandoned in the interest of the new national priorities. Social workers were more concerned with the lack of adequate child care and facilities than with the effects of employment itself. They assumed that the conditions that forced women to work during the war (i.e., the lack of manpower) would dissipate once the men returned from overseas. Although many women did retire to their homes after their husbands returned, others found they *enjoyed* working outside the home. Far from shrinking, the rate of maternal employment continued to rise!

During the midtwentieth century, studies regarding the effects of maternal employment began to resurface. Scholars focused upon intelligence, achievement, psychosocial adjustment, and attitudes of children whose mothers worked or did not work outside the home. While previous research seldom differentiated between male and female subjects, scholars began explicitly to study the contrasting effects of maternal employment on girls and boys. (Researchers noted positive, negative and neutral effects on both sexes.)

The findings of research can only be as accurate as the methods used in obtaining them. In a 1960 critique of maternal employment literature, Stolz recommended changes in the future research on the subject. Stolz pointed out that the definition of employment varied from one study to the next, making the research appear vague and inconsistent. Conditions of employment were often ignored by researchers who failed to differentiate by quantity or quality. In some studies women employed on a part-time basis were counted alongside full-time workers. Researchers sometimes included home-mothers with part-time employed mothers. In one study, the researcher advocated placing the home-mothers into the same group as the full-time employed mothers. Scholars frequently failed to identify type of employment such as labor, management or professional careers. Other sources of confusion identified by Stolz included the theorists' lack of attention to family variations: socioeconomic factors, the style of family relationships, and characteristics of the mothers such as their attitudes toward work and child rearing. Stolz suggested that imprecise definitions of these employment variables caused some of the inconsistent findings that plagued researchers.

DAUGHTERS AND MATERNAL EMPLOYMENT RESEARCH

Studies conducted since 1960 often failed to heed Stolz's recommendations. The number of working hours per week needed to qualify for full-time employment varied from twenty to forty-plus hours. Mothers could have worked outside the home for their daughter's entire childhood, or for as little as the day of the study. Similarly, previously employed women may have qualified to be classified as home-mothers if they happened to quit their jobs just before the investigation. Some researchers tried to control this confounding variable by including a specific time requirement such as six years of employment or nonemployment immediately prior to the study. However, researchers who used such requirements did not tend to account for the initial years of the daughters' lives.

Areas covered in the maternal employment studies include achievement of children, their attitudes, their psychosocial adjustment, and their interpersonal relationships (parents, friends, etc.), as listed in Table 2.1. Interpersonal relationships of the child and others have been of consistent interest to researchers in the last three decades. In contrast, studies regarding the development of attitudes such as sex role attitude development, self-efficacy, self-esteem, parenting attitudes, and educational and career aspirations took place primarily in the seventies and early eighties.

Exploration of children's achievement such as grades, intelligence quotients, and teacher perceptions were conducted in the sixties and seventies. Those studies typically noted insignificant or no differ-

Table 2.1
Areas of Research

Achievement	Attitudes
School Grades	Career
I.Q. scores	Parenting
School Performance	Sexual Identity

Psychosocial	Interpersonal-
Adjustment	Relationships
Personality	Parent-Child
Depression	Parent-Teenager
Stress	Peer Relationships

ences between the achievement, grades, and performance of the daughters of employed and those of nonemployed mothers. This is not very surprising since the enduring traits of intelligence and ability would likely not be affected by conditions other than severe limitations of nutrition or oxygen. Maternal employment, while presumably having some effect, was not by itself injurious enough to impair basic intelligence. The studies at the beginning of the twentieth century regarding the "retardation" of the children of working mothers were hopelessly confounded by the methodological inadequacies and cultural prejudices of the day. For instance, the category often included the children of immigrants because their grasp of English was not up to the grade level expected of a typical (same aged) American child. At the same time, children of immigrant parents were more likely to have mothers employed outside the home helping to support the family. Board members responsible for interpreting the study results lumped together all such children as "retarded" regardless of salient information suggesting alternative explanations.

The attitudes of the daughters of employed or nonemployed mothers were shown to be quite different. Daughters of employed mothers were found more likely to have the expectation to have a job outside the home while also rearing children, but one study indicated that they feared they would be unable to find suitable mates to marry or sustain a good marriage. Studies that examined the sex role attitude of children noted a tendency for the daughters of employed mothers to have more androgynous attitudes regarding the performance of tasks. Those researchers defined androgyny as the tendency to assume tasks regardless of socialized sexual expectations. Today, we know that the nurse may be a man and the doctor is very often a woman. However, despite the disintegration of long held stereotypes, the average person is still likely to envision a woman if the word "nurse" is stated or written and a man if the word "doctor" is used. In the same manner, some tasks are viewed as being masculine or feminine. For instance, diapering a baby, cleaning toilets, and grocery shopping may be the wife's jobs in some families while taking out the garbage, mowing the grass, and carving the Thanksgiving turkey are the husband's domain. When scholars studied girls of differing ages (five to fifteen years) concerning their attitudes about sex role task identification, they discovered that the daughters being reared by working mothers indicated that most tasks could be accomplished by either males or females. Daughters reared by home-mothers, on the other hand, generally viewed tasks in traditional stereotyped orientations. This may have developed because the girls reared by working mothers were more likely to witness their fathers doing traditionally feminine tasks in the home while the mother worked. At the same juncture, the daughters of working mothers may have witnessed more dominant behavior by their mothers such as displaying heightened self-esteem, telling the husband what needed to be done in the house and bringing home the bacon. Interestingly enough, although the daughters of employed mothers recognized that the traditionally masculine careers were open to them, they were just as unlikely to choose such a career for themselves as the daughters of home-mothers. The theorists who discovered that phenomenon suggested the girls realistically understood the difficulties inherent in breaking into a masculine profession or were confused by the large number of careers open to them. Despite this, girls reared by full-time employed mothers still tended to report higher academic and career aspirations than girls reared by home-mothers.

Typically, the daughters studied in various research studies were most comfortable with and expressed a belief in whatever their mother's choices reflected. If the mother was a home-mother, the daughter was more likely to support the home-mother role model while disparaging the working mother paradigm. In contrast, daughters of working mothers (who combined child rearing with careers) supported the life-style of their mothers. However, this pattern broke down in several instances. Teenage girls with working mothers verbalized a desire to have fewer children or no children at all when they grew up. When scholars studied older daughters who either were new parents or were old enough to think of becoming parents, subjects reared by full-time working mothers were more likely to state that their mother's working hurt them when they were small children. Both the daughters of full-time employed mothers and daughters of home-mothers expressed a reluctance to return to work full-time when their children were infants. Alternatively, the subjects reared by mothers who had worked part-time or later in the subject's lives (i.e., the teen years) stated that they had benefited from their mother's employment and that they intended to return to their careers earlier in their infants' lives.

> I wish I could financially afford to stay home with my daughter full-time until she reaches the age of two, and then put her in day care, instead of going back to work after 2 months. My aunt will be watching her when I go back to work. Unfortunately, in this day and age, it takes 2 incomes to make it financially. However, my career is also important to me, and my job is fairly flexible (Luckily!) (PM2)

> I've always worked full time. Had my baby at 36—went back full time with him at 6 weeks and even kept in touch with the office during my maternity leave. It's worked out great for both of us. Having my son gave me balance (so not 100% career oriented); being in day care has made him outgoing, well rounded, unselfish. He's so much nicer than the clingy, whiny kids I see from stay-at-home moms. I freely admit prejudice—this is the best way for me. He's learned so much from school. I have a lovable, happy kid. When I leave work now, I leave it (used to take it home). After work and weekends is all kids time!! (PM2)

Researchers studying the findings of literature on the effects of maternal employment on daughters have noted that they have been confusing and contradictory. Not only have scholars reviewing the studies found contrasting results for boys and girls, various studies have found conflicting results within each sex. In particular, the issue of personal adjustment has evinced contradictory findings. Studies using primarily standardized testing tended to find the daughters of employed mothers better adjusted psychologically than the daughters of home-mothers. On the other hand, studies employing observation and second party behavioral checklists were more likely to find the daughters of working mothers to be less well adjusted in comparison to the daughters of home-mothers. Bee (1978) suggested that the use of standardized tests, constructed with masculine values, might have raised confusion on the issue of mental health for females.

During the nineteen eighties and early nineties, the focus of research began to shift to relationship variables; a very different picture started to emerge for the daughters of women who worked outside the home. The enhanced expectation of stress for women who juggled career, home and parental duties became a salient topic for research. Daughters, in particular, seemed to be affected by the working mother's stress and work overload.

> I felt lonely & isolated—could not participate in a lot of the after-school activities my friends were in, and she was always tired in the evening. (FM1)

> It is one of the main reasons I do not work while my children are young. My mother focused so much of her energy into her job and personal fulfillment that she neglected us. She described a housewife/mother as a "god awful" thing to do. (PM1)

Daughters of employed mothers were found to be more emotionally removed from their fathers and mothers in homes where there were also significant amounts of anger and tension. Researchers found home-mothers had a closer relationship with their daughters, while working women were more likely to have closer relations with their sons.

> I was a very frightened latchkey kid—never had a relationship with either parent and had an enormous desire to have one. (PM1)

I have never felt especially close to her. Her job took a lot of her time and interest and appeared to be more important than her home life (although appearances were always important). My mother seemed (on the surface) to be able to do it all—a successful career, a lovely well-maintained home, and three "model" children. In reality, my youngest brother and I more or less raised ourselves. My other brother (between my little brother and me in age) got most of our mom's attention. He was and remains her favorite (best looking, smartest, most-athletic, etc. of the 3 of us). Because I was the oldest, and a girl, I had a lot of responsibility to do housework, cooking, etc. until my mother got home from work. (*FM1*)

These findings suggested that the daughters of women who had worked full-time outside the home benefited in some ways but suffered in others. Daughters reared by employed mothers displayed an understanding of an expectation for an egalitarian lifestyle. They also aspired to more education. However, when researchers turned their attention to interpersonal issues, the findings suggested that the daughters reared by mothers who had worked full-time outside of the home were deprived of significant positive relationships with either one or both of their parents.

Girls who did not watch their mothers do work or parenting activities as frequently as the daughters of home-mothers may have developed a reduced sense of competency or efficacy when faced with adult tasks, including the task of raising their own children (Bandura, 1991). If the healthy psychosocial development of females demands substantial interpersonal interaction with mothers during childhood and adolescence, then mothers' absence from the home as a result of employment may impair significant aspects of feminine development.

With two young children I feel like I can never get anything accomplished, they are always making demands on me and there is never time to do just what I want to do, which at this point even if I did have the time I no longer know what I'd want to do. (*PM2*)

I wish I had had more children. I wish I could stay home in the summer with my son. I always feel pulled by home/work responsibilities & always feel inadequate in both areas. (*PM2*)

My work inside the home is boring, repetitive, lonely. I miss the contact you have with adults at work, the conversation, the stimulation of a busy office, deadlines. At home it's pretty much the same day after day, cooking, washing, cleaning up. It never ends and it's a constant. At one point I did work part-time but this was difficult, getting ready without having a child spit-up on you. My husband having to juggle dinner since it was in the evening was very supportive but found it difficult dealing with the children. Things are complicated in our house a little more by the fact that we have twins 17 months, and an older daughter 3 1/2. I guess you do feel a great joy though in their smiling faces and can't help but love them ever so much. I also feel only a parent can give a child the love it really needs at this early age. My twins are also difficult children and I don't know if outside care would be able to handle them. It's extremely difficult for my husband and I at times and we love them. I'm anxiously awaiting the day they start pre-school and I can go back to work and possibly have grandparents watch them part of the day. This will break things up for me, the kids and the grandparents wouldn't feel as taxed caring for them for a whole day. They would enjoy them. I also feel the children will have become more independent by then and benefit from the social contact with other children. I feel I'll enjoy them more because I won't have to deal with them all day. I don't think people realize how much harder it is to stay home with your children. They demand so much attention. And it's a job you don't leave or get a break from. I put in way over 40 hours a week 7 days a week. There is always laundry to be done, shopping, etc. But I guess the cuddles, good-night kisses and bedtime stories we share make it all worthwhile. (*PM2*)

3

I Think I Can Versus I Think I Can't

We cannot always comprehend the threads of thought that tie us to our actions. Our conception of logic is conspicuously simple and yet insidiously complex. I remember, when I was very young, reading Little Red Riding Hood for school. My first grade teacher assigned a few pages of the story as homework. As an afterthought, Miss Burnett suggested we try reading "between the lines" to understand some of the underlying meaning (although for the life of me I cannot now imagine what deeper meaning there could be in that story). After hours of trying (it seemed like hours), I gave up in frustration. No matter how hard I looked, no hidden messages lurked between the printed lines. Knowing failure, I returned to school the next day hoping against hope that it was the book and not my eyes that were defective. Of course the teacher eventually explained what the phrase "read between the lines" meant. Even so, it occurred to me at the age of six that hidden messages were just not fair. To me, it seemed logical that the world was real, touchable and understandable.

As adults, we have learned that the meaning of life often exists not in what we perceive with our senses, but rather in what we do not perceive. These are the messages that underlie and direct our lives *because* we do not usually see or hear them. As an example, when we are prejudiced against a certain group or person because of gender, color or nationality, it is not necessarily because that person did anything to us. We are usually reacting to a message or event, long forgotten, that still influences our current attitudes and behaviors. Advertisers have long known the most powerful messages are subliminal cues. Such suggestions tell us without words that the more expensive automobile would make us feel richer (while actually making us poorer).

The influence these messages play in our lives weakens as we become aware of them. That is why we hope education about different peoples will help eradicate sexism, racism, and all other isms, in the same way consumer advocates hope that an informed shopper will be a smart customer.

Psychologists and psychiatrists are still learning about "hidden" messages. They have begun to unravel some of the mysteries of emotional disorders such as anorexia by realizing the strong effect a person's perception of him/herself has upon behavior. In the case of anorexia nervosa, the patient (usually female) believes she is too fat even as her bodily systems shut down from starvation. When the anorexic patient looks into a mirror, she "sees" a fat person. This is an extremely dangerous assumption with potentially lethal consequences. However, we all have preconceived notions and unconscious rationales that influence our lives in potent ways. The perception of self-efficacy is one such influence.

THE PERCEPTION OF SELF-EFFICACY

Imagine a book lying on the floor of the room you are in. In our society books do not generally sit in the middle of the floor, so you ask yourself, "Is it my responsibility to pick up the book?" Then you might wonder if you can pick up the book, "Do I have the time to do this?" Finally, you might pick up the book. The sequence you went through looked something like this:

Perception of a task→
Assumption of personal responsibility for the task→
Ability to carry out the task→
Carry out the task.

Table 3.1
Perception of Self-Efficacy and Books

```
H
I
G
H

L
O
W    Pick Up Book          Read Book                    Write Book
     SIMPLE<------------>MODERATE<------------>COMPLEX
```

At any point this decision making may have broken down. You could have decided not to see the book, that the book was not your responsibility, or that you were not able to spare the time or energy to retrieve it. The fate of the book depends upon the positive or negative completion of each stage of your decision making. On the surface, this sequence of decision making appears logical, and yet it is deceptively simple. "Between the lines" hide at least one decision making step that can also confound successful action. Although you may have the ability to pick up the book, you may not think you have book-picking-up-ability. This idea is the concept of *the perception of self-efficacy*. The sequence of decision making becomes:

Perception of a task→

Assumption of personal responsibility for the task→

Ability to carry out the task→

Perception of ability (self-efficacy) to carry out task→

Carry out the task.

For any action to be taken, the participant must feel capable of completing the task. The participant must feel self-efficacy.

Picking up a book from the floor is a very simple task for which most people have a high level of self-efficacy. Reading a book is a more complex task, however, that requires skills some have not mastered. Feelings of efficacy regarding reading depend upon the enjoyment of reading, the difficulty of the book, and the interest that particular book invokes. In comparison to reading a book, very few of us feel able to write a book (See Table 3.1).

As odd as it may seem, within an area such as "books," the ability to perform a complex task is not necessarily dependent upon the ability to perform simple tasks. For instance, an illiterate person may be able to "write" a book with the use of a tape recorder. Someone paralyzed by a stroke may not be physically able to open a volume but can read the book if another person assists by turning the pages.

In addition, the physical or mental ability to perform a task may be present, but if the individual feels incapable of that task, even the attempt to master it is less likely. How many wonderful books remain unwritten because the "author" did not feel able? We will never know.

What makes an able person feel able or unable to perform? Albert Bandura (1982) described efficacy as the tendency to believe that one is capable of performing a task. He indicated that the feeling of capability comes from four principal sources: (a) performance attainments, (b) vicarious experiences, (c) verbal persuasion, and (d) allied types of social influences.

Performance attainments are all the successes or failures an individual experiences in attempts at work, play, or relationships. When one tries a new activity such as playing a piano, the initial attempts may not be very encouraging. However, with practice, one can improve. It is the current and past success that help one feel as if more can be accomplished, that one is capable not only of present success but of future gains.

> I have chosen to be at home to raise my son. It has been a pleasure, a joy, a learning experience. I would not have traded this for any career. If you do a good job of raising kids and staying home, it is full-time. Sometimes I think I did it this way to see for myself that it could be done right and it could be satisfying. (*HM2*)

> I was home when they were toddlers and always try to have some quality time with them. I feel they all turned out well and have a good feeling about their futures. (*PM2*)

> This has worked out well. Our children are bright, happy, make friends easily, independent. They have seen their Dad performing traditional 'female" jobs, e.g., laundry, cooking, etc. (*FM2*)

Vicarious experiences are those times in life when people learn from watching others. When in a new social situation, people will commonly look to their companions to check out appropriate behavior. Then, they can behave similarly. By doing this, people learn to feel comfortable in many social situations. We commonly think of this experience as learning by someone else's mistakes, or not reinventing the wheel.

> She was my example. It was important to me that she was there. She always found being a wife, mother, and homemaker fulfilling, creative, busy and important. Her values were passed on to me. (*HM1*)

> Showed me how satisfying full time motherhood could be, allowed her children independence and security. Part-time work showed me you could do both. (*PM1*)

> I expected to grow up and work outside of the home for a living. (*FM1*)

Verbal persuasion is at work any time parents praise children for their attempts at a sport. Children are more likely to feel as if they can be good at that sport if the important people in their lives tell them they can. Verbal persuasion helps individuals have hope they can perform a task with increasing skill.

> Mom was always there; if she worked it was at home. She taught us what we needed, and to always try even if the odds were against us, to follow our heart but use our heads. We could always talk to her. She was our stability in life. (*HM1*)

> It made me proud of her when she worked outside the home. I learned to do many household tasks to help her and she always showed appreciation and praise to me for it. (*PM1*)

Whenever a portion of society mandates behavior by expectation, either helping or hindering an individual's perception of self-efficacy, *allied types of social influences* are present. Examples of this would be that girls can't do math and boys shouldn't cry. Physiologically, there is no reason why boys and girls cannot do both.

Habits and expectations combine to encourage one behavior over another.

I guess I didn't realize there were Moms who weren't at home. Back then, I took it for granted that she was always there. Today I appreciate it because I realize that some moms weren't always home. I think her being always there for me made me decide full-time work is not for me. I want my kids to be with me—not someone else! *(HM1)*

It can be very difficult to stay home. Less money, less value in society. But I have found volunteer work to fill part of the void. As far as my children go, I feel they are much better off than they would have been had I worked. I think it will be better for all of us when my youngest enters first grade. By then I'll be able to work part-time which, to me, seems to be the best situation for the family and me. *(PM2)*

Messages we have received from the world around us help us to perceive ourselves as others see us. The problem is, "others" may be wrong.

EFFICACY AND DAUGHTERS

There is a high potential for daughters to experience parenting, interpersonal relationships and management skills vicariously through their mothers. Daughters watch their mothers leading their own lives. They witness their mothers' successes in parenting, household tasks and relationships with their husbands.

The time I remember the most about my mother is not when I was small (although she was always at home for me), but when I was in high school. I don't know why, but I have such good memories of my high school years, coming home and calling out, "Mom I'm home"; she'd always call and tell me where she's at and we'd talk about my day or her day and what we were going to do that afternoon! The things I needed to get done or what we were doing that evening. It was a very good memory for me and [it] felt important for me at that time of my life as a teenager. I learned from her because we worked together, cleaning, gardening, cooking, helping others, etc. She had a big impact on my life. I feel that's why, I'm the way I am! The thing I saw most in my mother was, my father loved her. That tells me a lot, she had done something right for a man to love her like he did, and I think she showed me her secret by her life. (HM1)

The fact that my mother primarily stayed at home gave me a great sense of security growing up. However, with only one income, we had to make do with much less than others in the neighborhood. I think it shaped my feelings that I would be financially independent of a man. It was clear to me that my mother found her role very satisfying and fulfilling. I expected to also find my role as mother similarly fulfilling, and although I delayed children until my career was well established, I have found motherhood to be a fulfilling new dimension in my life. (PM1)

On the other hand, daughters may also have observed their mothers failing at the demands of employment and/or motherhood.

My mother felt "trapped" and referred to herself as "an artist" who gave up career because of marriage and children. She felt her life was very hard. She never worked even when money troubles were desperate; she never even had a vegetable garden, though she grew flowers. I wish she had been less martyred; we paid for her "sacrifice." She'd have been gentler if "fulfilled." (HM1)

My mother was inadequate inside and outside the home. She could never handle having a job outside the home and would become very anxious and upset all the time due to the added stress of employment. When she was a full time mother her housekeeping was horrible. All six of my brothers and sisters were physically abused and neglected. (PM1)

Reflecting back it's (mother's working) probably the best that could have happened. As a result I was raised/cared for by great Grandmo[ther] and grandfather ages birth to 7 and with

Aunt, Uncle and 2 boy cousins 4–10. Paternal relatives who
were healthier so it balanced out the abusive behavior. The
most difficult years were the ones she was at home with my
2 adopted brothers and she was there when I came home from
school. (FM1)

According to the efficacy theory, if mothers are capable at parenting, marriage and career tasks, the daughters are more likely to
feel enhanced skills in those areas because of the verbal reinforcement, teaching of homemaking skills, and vicarious learning taking
place.

In the nineties, fewer daughters have the opportunity to watch
their mothers for significant periods of time in the home. Fewer
mothers are able to or decide to stay home. Less than one-third of
married women with children under the age of eighteen were still
at home as of 1991. As reported by the U.S. Bureau of the Census,
67.8% of married women with children were employed outside the
home (1993). However, the reality of the working mother has not
yet reached the mainstream of American consciousness (The Gallup
Poll Monthly, 1991, 1990). Mothers who choose to work outside the
home while rearing young children are still seen as non-traditional
and often have little support from allied types of social influences.
Society and families alike often fail to give the physical and emotional
support working women need. Sometimes women find that their
children's traditional "grandmother" provides no support or respect
for her working daughter. "Grandmother" may strongly disapprove
of her daughter's choice of employment outside the home.

On the basis of the labor statistics from 1948 to 1975 (the years
baby boomers were likely still to be in the home) the average maternal employment rose from 26.0% to 52.3%. What this suggests
is that a woman who was born in those years has better than a fifty-
fifty chance (during any given year) of having had an at-home mother
as a role model. Many women who work outside the home while
raising their own families must do so without the benefit of their
mother's modeling how to juggle family and career needs.

Good positive role model for being a wife and mother. No role
model for achievement, competency, independence or earning

a living, low expectations for girls/women; get married, have children. (*HM1*)

I liked her being at home when I was growing up. It was nice for her to be there when I got home from school. She was very dependent though and I think her self esteem and mine would have been higher if she had worked outside home. (*HM1*)

She *never* worked other than as a housewife and mother—she doesn't "understand" that I have a commitment to my job and thinks I should be in the home full-time. (*HM1*)

On the other hand, women whose mothers worked outside the home while they were young may not know how to be stay-at-home mothers.

Mother was a professional and ambitious, energetic hard-worker, good role model. But when I tried to be a stay-at-home mom (for the sake of my children) I found I didn't know how to do that, found it *very* stressful. (*FM1*)

Once the pertinent questions for the Sugar Study evolved, my advisers (Rita and Fred) asked me what, in my opinion, the results were likely to be. The answer I gave them seemed quite logical at the time. I assumed:

- The subjects would not differ significantly in their self-perception of general efficacy or any other major factor such as depression, stress, life satisfaction, or interpersonal relationships with their spouses.
- The daughters reared by home-mothers would feel more efficacious in the parenting role.
- The daughters reared by employed mothers would feel more efficacious in their careers and ability to combine their family and career.

Here's what I found out.

Table 3.2
Perception of General Self-Efficacy

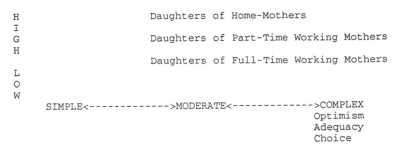

```
H                        Daughters of Home-Mothers
I
G                        Daughters of Part-Time Working Mothers
H
                         Daughters of Full-Time Working Mothers
L
O
W
     SIMPLE<------------->MODERATE<------------->COMPLEX
                                                 Optimism
                                                 Adequacy
                                                 Choice
```

THE SUBJECT'S PERCEPTION OF GENERAL SELF-EFFICACY

Contrary to my initial assumptions, the findings of the study suggested a significant relationship between maternal employment and reduced sense of complex general self-efficacy for the subjects reared by full-time employed mothers (see Table 3.2).

The discovery that women reared by full-time employed mothers felt less efficacious in general confirmed the findings of other studies that used younger girls as subjects. The teenage daughters of full-time working mothers also experienced more feelings of insecurity and inadequacy than the daughters of home-mothers in one study. In another study, the adolescent daughters of full-time employed mothers were more likely to worry about their abilities to find suitable mates and have successful marriages in the future. In yet another study, the daughters of employed mothers saw themselves as less able to have an impact on their world.

In the Sugar Study, the women reared by full-time working mothers displayed significantly less optimism, felt less satisfaction with their general adequacy, and (along with women reared by part-time working mothers) were significantly less likely to believe that they had a choice in whether or not they worked outside the home.

Figure 3.1 graphically illustrates how the subjects reared by full-time employed mothers felt more neutral and pessimistic about their lives. Subjects reared by part-time employed women also felt less optimistic than subjects in the home-mother group.

Why the daughters of employed women felt less optimism than

Figure 3.1
Pessimism Scale

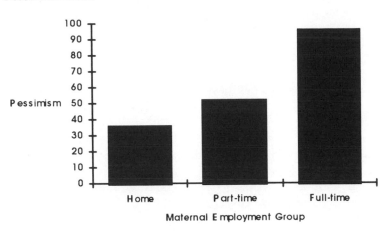

Maternal Employment Group

the daughters of home-mothers is unclear. Even the subjects reared by part-time employed mothers expressed more neutral and pessimistic feelings on average than the daughters of home-mothers, albeit not significantly more. Perhaps the mothers who remained in the home to rear their daughters provided the security and unconditional acceptance the girls felt they needed or wanted as they grew to womanhood. Subjects in the home-mothers' group were likely to say about their mothers, "I had a very secure feeling because Mom was there" and "Having Mom at home made me feel secure, happy, and loved." On the other hand, the daughters reared by full-time employed mothers more often reported, "I felt lonely and isolated" and "I felt cheated." Not all the comments made by the women reared by full-time working mothers were negative. One daughter of a working mother wrote this:

Inside the home—[Mom] showed me the importance of concern and caring for others—[she provided a] caregiver model—very loving[.] love [is shown] through food also.

Outside the home—[Mom provided a] professional role model—[she was a] hard worker, dedicated worker—[She showed the] possibility of success, professional image in appearance, importance of doing the job completely and well

both when working inside and outside home—showed that the
father/husband would share in household chores; managed
money together. Showed me the mother and father sharing
common interests when working. Showed me the satisfaction
she got from her work and the love of her career while also
taking great interest in family. (*FM1*)

However, in the study questionnaire, this particular subject evinced
the same markers that characterized so many of the subjects in the
full-time employment group. Her questionnaire revealed that she
felt pessimistic, worried about her ability to handle future problems
of her children, and less satisfied with her life. She also indicated
her perception of paternal mental incapacitation while she was growing up. For the most part, the daughters of full-time employed
mothers reported *negative* emotions of fear and loneliness or neutral
comments about learning to manage time or household tasks when
discussing about their childhood.

I felt neglected & disappointed she wasn't home like my
friends' mothers although I knew she had to work to support
the family. (*FM1*)

I felt lonely & isolated—could not participate in a lot of the
after-school activities my friends were in, and she was always
tired in the evening. (*FM1*)

I learned independence in getting up and ready for school,
then preparing dinner after school. I missed having that done
for me like other mothers did. (*FM1*)

—I was fearful as a "latchkey" child.
—I resented having to take care of the household chores
   (but I always tended to be careless about housekeeping).
—I was lonely and isolated.
—It made me learn to rely on myself. (*FM1*)

The daughters of home-mothers reported more security and
happiness:

My mother stayed home to raise 7 children—that was a vocation. Now that the children are married, my mother works

as a receptionist in my father's office. It was great having the secure feeling of having a parent at home—to listen, to care for, to share with us and guide us. I am glad I am able to stay at home to raise our children—there's much to be said for the parent "being there" for their children. (*HM1*)

Having Mom at home made me feel secure, happy, and loved. (*HM1*)

I was the sixth of seven children. She was always there, although very busy. She constantly worked or read or played games (card solitaire). I felt very fortunate to have so much exposure to a wonderful person. (*HM1*)

I loved having my mom home—knowing she'd be there when I came home everyday was a great feeling. (*HM1*)

The findings of this study suggest the perceived lack of security and stable emotional support (reported by the subjects reared by full-time employed mothers) left those subjects with lowered self-esteem and reduced perceptions of self-efficacy. The subjects reared by full-time employed mothers seemed to have felt they were less important—a lower priority. Said one:

I grew up feeling like I got lost in the shuffle. I feel like if she had been home, and not working, she might have seen how I felt rejected, unloved and worthless. And maybe I would have gotten professional help while I was younger. (*FM1*)

THE PERCEPTION OF CHOICE

The perception of choice is also a necessary condition for the perception of self-efficacy. People who feel efficacious are in a powerful condition. They know that they have control over their own situations and can perform tasks with skill. However, if individuals feel they have little or no choice over a major portion of their daily routine, they have less power to make changes or control their lives. Therefore, the perception of choice is necessary for self-efficacy. The daughters of employed mothers, whether the mothers worked part-time or full-time, were two and a half to three times more likely

Figure 3.2
Perceived Lack of Choice by Maternal Employment Group

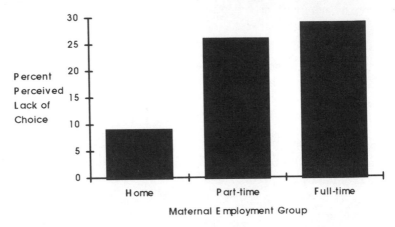

to report having little or no choice whether they worked inside or outside the home as adults (See Figure 3.2).

The demographic data obtained for the study did not suggest a compelling reason why so many more of the 163 subjects reared by employed mothers felt a lack of choice in comparison to the 90 subjects in the home-mother group. It may have been that the daughters reared by home-mothers were better able to withstand the financial and social pressures involved in leaving home for employment or staying home with children, because they witnessed their mother's coping in the home.

> I'm glad my mom was always home. I was the oldest of 5 and my mom needed to be home to handle the demands of 5 kids. She never wanted to work outside the home. Having her always there was a very secure thing for us. My mother was always home when I needed her. Her strong support still continues today. I feel that because she was home—I now have a strong sense of self, self-confidence and a very positive attitude towards life. My relationships with others are strong and non-demanding. (*HM1*)

> Her example and her words affected my decisions to work or not, to stay home. Most important I think I was able to stay

home without feeling like less of a person (a message our society sends) because I saw enormous value in what she did. I truly believe raising kids is a full time job and the most important job in the country. (*HM1*)

Perhaps the lack of a home-mother role model made the daughters of employed mothers feel less capable in the home. Subjects who had employed mothers while growing up frequently reported their lack of ease in the home or a psychological or social need to work. In addition, the daughters of working mothers may have received explicit verbal messages from their mothers that they had no choice but to work outside the home. The daughters could have translated that cue into the belief that no mother had a choice but to work outside the home.

I always felt I should do more than just stay home—my mother was never happy just parenting. (*PM1*)

I think I always assumed I would work for a living. Not especially when the kids were young, but for most of my adult life. I knew I was supposed to go to college and to get a good job, etc. By high school/college I knew it was economically unlikely to be able to stay home and raise kids, so I assumed I would work then also. (*PM1*)

Some previous studies did not find significant psychosocial differences between daughters of home-mothers and daughters of full-time working mothers. One possible explanation for the lack of such findings could be that the perception of self-efficacy is an accumulation of all childhood experiences; studies using young adolescents or children may not have been sufficiently sensitive to discern incipient psychosocial gaps. In addition, the consequences of maternal employment may have had a sleeper effect that remained obscure until the daughter was older and expected by society to live as an adult. Because women struggle with demands of children, husbands, chores, and career choice (whether inside or outside the home), the effect of their mother's employment decision may become magnified as everyday demands increase. Unlike the younger subjects of studies in the past, the women in the present study have had considerable responsibilities in their work, marital, and parental roles.

Many researchers have investigated the enduring traits of intelligence and personality when studying the effects of maternal employment. The presence or absence of mothers as a result of employment may have had little or no impact upon those stable traits. In contrast, the subjects' perceptions of self-efficacy appear to have been more sensitive to the demands and limitations made by working mothers. It may be that previous research simply did not ask the right questions. If teenage daughters were asked about their feelings of choice, child rearing and accomplishments, we might see answers that are the same as or similar to those of the more mature women of this study.

Finally, the use of standardized intelligence tests normed on males may have given a false indication of superior personal adjustment for the daughters of working women. The subject of personal adjustment invokes the most baffling contradiction within the literature of the effects of maternal employment. While several studies noted greater adjustment for the daughters of employed women, several others found daughters of working mothers more maladjusted than the daughters of home-mothers. One reason for such divergent results may have been the behavioral measures used in the studies. Generally, the studies that found positive results for daughters of employed mothers utilized standardized tests, while research that had negative findings for girls reared by employed mothers tended to have used observation or second party behavioral checklists. Helen Bee (1978) provided information relevant to this issue. In her overview on sex differences of children, she raised serious questions about the wisdom of using standardized tests on girls because they often used group norms that included boys and typically had masculine assumptions of psychological health. Bee discussed the presupposition of test creators, who found masculine ideals of independence, assertiveness and competition as universally desirable for females as for males:

Psychologists, social workers, and other health professionals rate the healthy adult and the healthy male in similar ways, but the healthy female is *not* seen as having the same qualities as the healthy adult. Thus generally desirable characteristics for *any* adult are likely to be stereotypically male qualities. In some sense, the more a woman conforms to the female stereotype, the less likely she is thought of as "healthy" by mental-health professionals. (pp. 20–21)

Using such logic in the construction of standardized tests, the scores of the most well adjusted girls would resemble those of boys in attitude and personality. The impact of using tests with masculine ideals and norms could have had a confusing influence upon the findings in some research studies that found more positive adjustment for the daughters of employed mothers.

One of the few areas of maternal employment literature that have shown consistent results is sexual role identification. Studies have repeatedly shown that daughters of employed mothers appeared more androgynous, showing more attitudes and behaviors that resemble those of boys, more than daughters reared by home-mothers. The assumption of better psychological adjustment of the daughters of working mothers as shown by standardized tests (in some studies) may be unwarranted. Instead, it may indicate that the daughters of working women psychologically resemble boys. However, that may not be a marker of good psychological health for girls.

While few researchers have studied the results of maternal employment for adolescents, the Canadian study conducted by Burke and Weir (1978) suggests in conclusion:

It would be quite realistic to assume that working mothers, in carrying job responsibilities in addition to household responsibilities, might have reduced energy and time to provide the cognitive and emotional dimensions necessary to meet the needs of their still dependent daughters. If this is not forthcoming from the mothers and no significant other is perceived as a potential provider of the required nurturance and confirmation, then feelings of insecurity and inadequacy may ensue. (p. 1169)

FEELING (IN)ADEQUATE

The subjects in the present study felt less adequate (in general) if their mothers had employment full-time for more than eight years during their childhood. In this particular instance, however, the

Figure 3.3
Level of Subject Dissatisfaction with Her General Adequacy

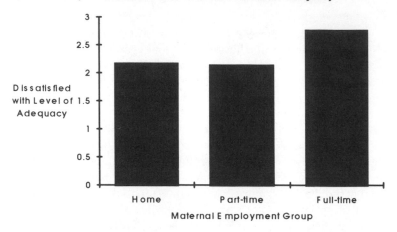

Maternal Employment Group

daughters of part-time employed mothers fared slightly better than the subjects reared by home-mothers (see Figure 3.3).

The statistical analysis (which reached significance) revealed the following levels of dissatisfaction for the subjects (lower scores suggest more satisfaction with perception of general feelings of adequacy):

Subjects reared by home mothers	2.17
Subjects reared by part-time employed mothers	2.14
Subjects reared by full-time employed mothers	2.77

The difference in effects of maternal employment between girls and boys in adolescence may be a reflection of the differing psychosocial needs of each sex. Gecas and Schwalbe (1986) examined the relationship between parental behavior and children's perceptions of parental behavior. They mailed questionnaires to 128 adolescents (seventeen to nineteen years of age) and their parents to learn about the adolescents' perception of their parents' parenting and the teens' feelings of self-esteem and efficacy. They found the boys' perception of self-efficacy more affected by the level of control or autonomy of the parents. In contrast, the girls' level of self-efficacy varied, depending on parental support and interaction (particularly the father's). What this means is that girls felt more able to perceive they could handle their world well, or efficaciously, if their mothers and fathers spent more time with them in talking, providing emotional support, and giving overall attention. The less time parents spent with their daughters in psychosocial interaction, the less capable the girls felt about their lives.

PERCEPTION OF GLOBAL SATISFACTION

Some theorists have suggested that adolescents prefer mothers to work outside the home so that the children can have greater autonomy and increased financial benefits. Other studies, however, have shown that maternal employment produced a reduction in children's global satisfaction. Brenda Hunter in *Home by Choice* (1991) wrote from personal experience:

> But not all children like coming home to empty houses. I didn't. From the age of seven onwards I came home to an empty apartment after school. . . . I was grateful on those occasions when mother was home after school. Unfortunately, she would often have to walk back to work while I kept my lonely and frightening vigil at home alone, sometimes until ten o'clock at night. (p. 104)

Just as with the perception of general adequacy, the subjects who felt the most satisfied with their lives were those whose mothers had been home-mothers or who had part-time employment. Lower scores suggest more satisfaction with life.

Subjects reared by home mothers	2.05
Subjects reared by part-time employed mothers	2.09
Subjects reared by full-time employed mothers	2.42

In summary, the subjects reared by home-mothers felt significantly better about themselves and their lives than the subjects

Figure 3.4
Level of Dissatisfaction with Life Noted for Subjects

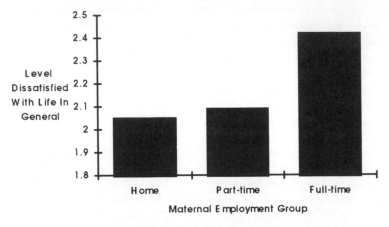

Note: Scores of 1 and 2, respectively, indicated very satisfied or satisfied.

reared by full-time employed mothers (see Figure 3.4). The daughters reared by part-time employed mothers had a mixed set of scores. Although they scored better than the subjects reared by full-time employed mothers, they felt less optimism in their lives than the daughters of home-mothers and scored very similarly to the subjects reared by full-time employed mothers in that they more often believed they had little or no choice in whether they worked outside the home.

I loved my mother being there when I came home from school. If she had an appointment and was not there things were not right until she got there. Even if verbal communication was not there, having her physically near by was comforting. Anyway no one I knew had a "working" mother, that would be out of the ordinary. (*HM1*)

I always admired my mother and wanted to be like her. I was always glad she was home. We never had much money but there was plenty of love. My Mom was always available. During the two years she worked in the school cafeteria, I hated it. She was home when I left for school and when I got home, but somehow I hated the idea that she wasn't there. It doesn't make sense, but that's the way I felt. I always felt that my mother was a worthwhile person who was contributing to society by the way she raised me and my brother and how she gave to her family. I never thought of this as not having a career. When a school counselor asked what I wanted to do "when you grow up" I said "a wife and mother." I was told that was not an option. I had to go to college and have a career. I felt very insulted for my mother. I knew she was a very intelligent person who had one of the most worthwhile careers. My mother was a wonderful role model. She never tried to influence my career choice. She would have supported me whatever my choice. (*PM1*)

4

How Do Mothers Feel About Themselves?

At a little over eight months of pregnancy it suddenly occurred to me that I was really going to give birth to an infant. More than that, I finally comprehended the irreversibility of my condition (to most women this realization comes much sooner in the nine months!!). There could be no change of mind! That flash of knowledge left me so upset I gave birth the very next day, three weeks early, to our first daughter. Twenty months later, there was little fear or worry when I gave birth to our second daughter. Familiarity with the birth process and knowing I could care for a newborn infant helped me feel relaxed and confident. Having a child was a snap. However, as any veteran parent knows, overwhelming fear for a child's well-being can arise with every unfamiliar stage of development, every bump in the night, and each second in every hour of darkness spent waiting for a teenager to pull into the driveway.

Those of us who have completed parenting (though my mother said "It's never completed!") or are actively involved in parenting know that the good or even adequate mother is not the person who sits proudly at the high school graduation; it is the woman who suffers the pain with her children, while permitting them to make their own mistakes. The good mother is the woman who stands up

Table 4.1
Perception of Child-Rearing Self-Efficacy

```
H
I
G
H


L
O
W

   Feed Child            Love Child            Discipline Child
      SIMPLE<------------->MODERATE<------------->COMPLEX
```

to the wrath of a two-year-old toddler or teenage tyrant while re-maining flexible enough to realize she might even be wrong.

PARENTING SKILLS

There are a thousand answers to every parenting question and no absolutely correct solution. How amazing it is that children have been reared for millions of years when experts have been around for only a century or two! Consider the vast range of skills needed to rear a child in today's world. Women often take on the roles of teachers, nurses, diagnosticians, therapists, chauffeurs, cooks, and activity directors, among other identities. A *Mom*, however, is a being with an identity all her own. Mom is that person, whether she gave birth to you or not, who cared for you in every sense of the word. She may not always have felt comfortable in her role as mother. Indeed, she probably often felt like being cared for by her own mother in times of stress or sadness. How did she learn to become that all-important person? Mothering efficacy involves a variety of tasks with differing levels of complexity (see Table 4.1). In fact, the tasks of motherhood, or how they are performed, alter whenever the developmental needs of the child change. How on earth can anyone learn to become a mother when there are no hard and fast rules?

Girls learn how to become good mothers from many sources: daughters may baby-sit or care for younger siblings to gain expertise (performance attainments).

I felt quite experienced as a parent before my oldest daughter was born—I often mistakenly call her by my little sister's name. (*PM1*)

From their mother's example, girls learn intrinsically how to feel about mothering and the tasks involved in rearing a child (vicarious experience).

I was very glad she was home when I was little. There was security and stability in my family. I worked outside the home for almost 12 years. When we had a family—I chose to stay home to be with my children. My childhood influenced that choice. I feel it's important. (*HM1*)

The girls get encouragement or discouragement about child rearing from family, friends, or acquaintances (verbal persuasion).

As a single mother, now, and full time student I often get overwhelmed at the demands made on my personal life. My mother increases this guilt by reinforcing the idea that I should always do more for my kids. Overall I think my children understood my pressures and have turned out well so far and I hope they will follow their own heart when making choices like these instead of acting out of guilt, tradition, fear, spousal pressure, etc. (*HM2*)

I realize that there are many mothers who must work. I also believe it is fine for a mother to work outside the home if it works for her family; but I very much resent being told that I am somehow a less worthwhile person because I choose to stay home. (And I have been told that!) Where would some children be, and where would the schools be, if there were no "stay-at-home" Moms to help out? (*PM2*)

Girls are bombarded with messages from the outside world that tell them how wonderful or awful parenting is (allied types of social influences).

Contrary to what many "working" mothers and "experts" say, my children are very mature and self-reliant. Our house may

Figure 4.1
Worry About Ability to Handle Children's Problems

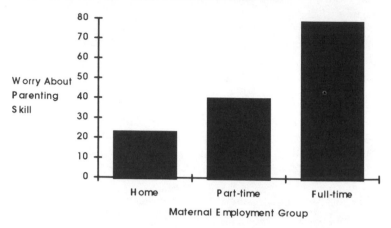

be small and cramped (3 bedrooms, 1 bath, no basement or garage) and pretty messy most of the time, but it is full of love. We have all made sacrifices financially and mentally for me to stay home, but we are all very happy with the decision. I am happy. (*PM2*)

SUBJECTS' PERCEPTIONS OF THEIR PARENTING SKILLS

When asked to indicate how well they had done in rearing their own children, the subjects reared by home-mothers and part-time employed mothers answered significantly more often that they had done well in the past and expected to do well in the future. Subjects reared by full-time employed mothers reported more concerns about their ability to handle parenting problems or felt they had already failed with parenting their children (see Figure 4.1). The average scores of the subjects reared by part-time employed mothers fell between those of the other two groups.

A reason for the difference of scores among the three maternal employment groups might be that the daughters reared by full-time employed mothers missed learning about the more complex tasks of parenthood such as discipline because of their mothers' absences (see Table 4.2).

Table 4.2
Perception of Parenting Self-Efficacy

```
H                         Daughters of Home-Mothers
I
G                         Daughters of Part-Time Working Mothers
H
                          Daughters of Full-Time Working Mothers
L
O
W
     SIMPLE<------------->MODERATE<------------->COMPLEX
                             Handle Children's Problems
                                 Parenting Skills
                          Rearing Children As Parents Did
```

Adolescents are often perceived as being adults without legal rights. Twelve-year-old children frequently have responsibility for the care of younger children and infants. Teens may hold down jobs while in high school and be expected to assume household tasks such as cleaning, shopping and cooking. Although girls may be able to handle the instrumental tasks of adulthood while very young, lack of sufficient support and guidance from their parents could mean they are missing crucial elements required for mature psychosocial development.

The tendency for working mothers to expect young daughters to perform the simpler instrumental roles of parenting such as cleaning, cooking, and caring for siblings may also deprive them of adequate parenting. The impact of maternal employment and the demands upon the adolescent daughter are still being determined. The subjects provide some information about the situation:

I resented the fact that I had to take charge when my mother was gone. I had ironing, cooking, all the cleaning, and charge of my brothers and sisters of which there were 1 older and 6 younger. I also resented the fact that when she was home, there were enough things to do and there never seemed to be enough time for me. (FM1)

My mother began working part-time evening shift as a nurse when I was 10. I still remember feelings of desertion and loneliness. As I got older, I would wait up until 1:00 a.m. just to talk to her. I also remember her being tired and stressed. The good side was—I had to bear the responsibility of making sure the family had dinner and the kitchen was cleaned, etc. I also realized we needed the money. My mother and I are best friends and have always been close. During my teenage years we drifted apart and I do blame her job obligations for this. (*PM1*)

The subjects reared by full-time employed mothers may have felt a resentment for the premature role of "parent" and homemaker that influenced their attitudes about parenting.

The most pronounced effect of my mother's returning to work was that I was given a lot of responsibility for my siblings (I was sixteen, they were 4–14). I felt abandoned. More strongly, I felt that they'd been abandoned. I felt over-burdened. I learned responsibility and developed a deep parental love for them because of the experience. (*PM1*)

They may also have had insufficient experience witnessing their mothers' parenting in the home.

In the second significant item of the parenting variable, the daughters of full-time working mothers were more likely to express dissatisfaction with their parenting skills than the subjects reared by home-mothers (see Figure 4.2). Obviously, this item was linked to the first one, about parenting. Again, the subjects reared by full-time employed mothers revealed their uneasiness with their skills for parenting.

In the graph, the highest "bar" indicates the most dissatisfaction with parenting skills. The subjects reared by full-time employed mothers feel less satisfied with their parenting skills. Although not as visually dramatic as many of the other graphs, after statistical analysis this item proved to be significant.

Data from the Sugar Study showed that women reared by full-time working mothers differed significantly in the perception of parenting efficacy from women whose mothers did not have employment outside the home while the daughters were children. When rearing their own children, the subjects reared by full-time employed mothers seemed to be at a disadvantage because they had less opportunity to develop a positive perception of parenting through watching their mothers on a day by day basis. The subjects

Figure 4.2
Level of Subjects' Dissatisfaction with Their Parenting Skills

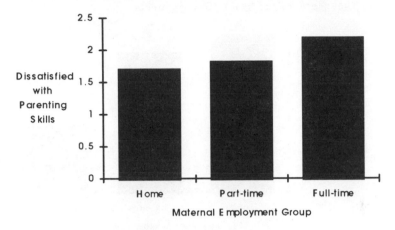

Maternal Employment Group

reared by full-time working mothers may also have received less verbal support for parenting from their mothers (when focusing upon the subjects' children), because the grandmothers may have found external employment more gratifying than parenting. Results from the present study suggest the existence of perceived unfilled psychosocial needs in daughters whose mothers worked outside the home for more than eight years during the first eighteen years of the subjects' lives.

PASSING ON THE TORCH

The third significant item in the perception of parenting efficacy indicated a difference among the three maternal employment groups concerning the similarity between their child rearing practices and the way the subjects' parents raised them. Only 19% of the daughters of full-time employed mothers reported they were rearing their children as their parents brought them up. In comparison, 44% of the women who had home-mothers (see Figure 4.3) indicated that they were rearing their children pretty much the way the (grand)parents raised them.

My mother mostly always worked and while my other friends went home to a "stay-at-home" mother and had home-made

Figure 4.3
Percent of Subjects Who Stated They Were Rearing Their Children Like They Were Raised by the (Grand)parents

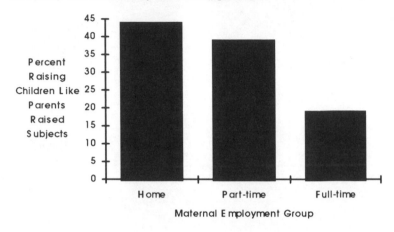

cookies waiting for them, I went home to an empty house after school. I swore I wouldn't do that to my children. That's why I stay at home with them. (*FM1*)

I want to be here for them. It's worth it. I wish my mom and I could have spent more of my childhood together (*FM1*)

In contrast, more of the women in the home-mother group expressed a desire to pass on family values and attitudes:

My fondest times as a child/teen were home with my mom and dad. I feel I turned out to be a pretty good, well adjusted adult because of her, so I feel I want to do the same for my kids. I can always work outside the home later on in life. (*HM1*)

I hope to pass the legacy of security and love I received from my own parents on to my own (children). (*HM1*)

ATTITUDES ABOUT PARENTING

Previous studies that explored the attitudes and sex role development of girls found some trends: two studies found an increased desire among the daughters of working mothers to remain childless (Farley, 1969; Rollins and White, 1982). The present study did not address the issue of childlessness because of the requirement that subjects be mothers. However, the increased difficulty that the subjects in the full-time maternal employment group reported in parenting their children, coupled with the increased desire of teenage girls (in other studies) to remain childless, suggests an impairment in the perception of parenting efficacy beginning, at least, in adolescence.

> I want my children to be good and listen and I am very stern at times. I wear down easily with my 2 wild boys and I'm inconsistent in my discipline, which I always feel bad about. When I was young I never could realize how a mother would not want to stay at home with her children. After 6 years of doing it, I'm ready to go back to work part time. It's a real chore keeping the house clean and can be depressing. I read lots of books and ask people advice on raising children and discipline. I have a few things going well but find DISCI-PLINE the hardest. On what to do at times—I feel very bad for a long time when I feel I haven't done the right thing (Pray a lot!). (PM47)

Several researchers found a blurring of sex roles in the way the daughters of employed mothers viewed themselves in career and family roles; the daughters of employed mothers also had less stereotypical views about women's roles in society (androgyny). The finding of androgyny in children and adolescents may not indicate a new type of life-style but instead may point to an undifferentiated sex role or lack of a firm identity. Daughters may *need* to attach themselves to a feminine role during adolescence for definitive sex role identification; however, as the career demographics in the present study have shown, this attachment did not mean that the girls were "trapped" forever in traditional feminine roles or occupations.

In past studies concerned with parenting attitudes and maternal employment, few effects surfaced. Amstey and Whitbourne (1988) discovered that the daughters of full-time working women were reluctant to return to work and expressed greater concern that children suffered from their mother's employment; subjects in that study were new parents who had little experience with long-term parenting. The employment status demographic in the Sugar Study was contrary to the attitudes of the daughters of full-time working mothers in the Amstey and Whitbourne study. Subjects reared by full-time employed mothers in the present study were *more* likely to be working (76%) than either the subjects in the home-mother (53%) or part-time (64%) maternal employment group.

How do you feel about the work you do in the home, child raising, and/or housework?

a. The only thing I wanted to do—completely fulfilling

b. It is OK, but I will be glad when the kids grow up and move out

c. Not rewarding or fulfilling—a lot of drudgery

d. Mixed feelings—some good, some not so good

e. I'm glad I stayed home with the kids especially when they were little

f. I'm glad I have a career outside the home

g. Not applicable

h. Other (please explain)

The preceding question was asked of the subjects regarding attitudes about their roles as housewives and mothers. Among other responses, it included an answer that provided the subjects with a tongue-in-cheek alternative. The response "f" to the homemaking question simply stated that the subject was glad to be outside the home. However, notice the percentage of subjects selecting that as their answer (see Figure 4.4). The striking pattern evident among the three maternal employment groups seems to indicate that subjects reared by full-time working mothers were less comfortable in the roles of homemaker and mother than the other subjects.

The intentions of the daughters reared by full-time employed mothers may have changed when they faced the long-term and seldom rewarded nature of careers as housewives and mothers.

I felt I need something outside the home because I became too reclusive. Not out going enough. Needing a way to meet other people (*FM2*)

Figure 4.4
Percent of Subjects Who Reported Being Happier to Work Outside the Home

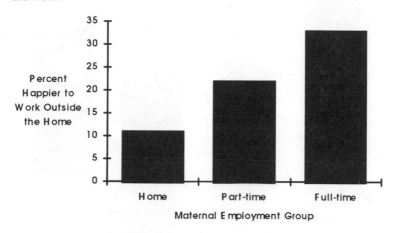

Maternal Employment Group

My job also brings me validation. I'm good at what I do and I really have needed that. (*FM2*)

Subject responses to the second open-ended question that asked how they felt about their work and how working affected their child rearing were quite interesting. The subjects reared by full-time employed mothers showed a psychological need (rather than just financial need or personal desire) to work outside the home (see Figure 4.5).

In stark contrast, the subjects reared by part-time employed mothers and home-mothers were far more likely to indicate highly positive attitudes about homemaking and child rearing (see Figure 4.6).

I know that I want to be able to stay at home at least until my children are in school. I'm even considering home schooling, so my desire to get back to work "outside" is very small right now. I'm very fulfilled in my role as wife and mother. (*PM2*)

By providing a secure, stable and attractive home for my family and our guests and guiding the physical/spiritual/emotional health and moral character of my children, I believe I am

Figure 4.5
Percent of Subjects Who Indicated a Psychological Need to Work Rather than Working for Enjoyment or for Economic Need

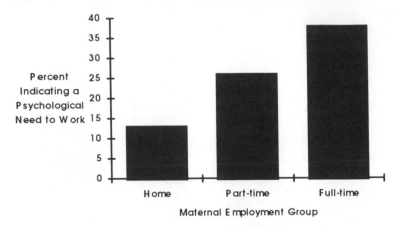

Figure 4.6
Percent of Subjects Who Stated They Were Completely Fulfilled by Their Role of Homemaker

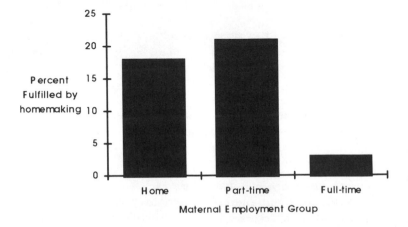

doing as much or more for our community and for posterity than I could in any other "career." No question this job has its share of drudgery—whose doesn't?—and is not without sacrifice, but it is challenging, stimulating and rewarding. (HM2)

In a previous study regarding the effects of maternal employment upon women, Wilson (1991) found no significant differences in androgyny among daughters whose mothers had been home-mothers, blue-collar workers or white-collar workers. Wilson's study included mothers who were older and more experienced, but did not have a "pure" home-mothers' group. This finding suggests decreasing differences (between girls whose mothers worked and girls who had home-mothers) regarding acceptance of nontraditional sex roles (androgyny) as they became adults. The finding may also mean that the higher "androgyny" levels measured by previous theorists actually indicated undifferentiated sex roles in adolescent girls. For women, an undifferentiated sex role correlates with confusion, aloofness, dissatisfaction, distrust and withdrawal (Peterson, Baucom, Elliott, and Farr, 1989).

PARENTING AND CAREERS

Past findings in the maternal employment literature suggested that daughters of full-time working mothers have an advantage in terms of future employment because they aspired to participate in careers and higher education more frequently than the daughters of home-mothers. The present study found the subjects reared by full-time employed women felt less efficacious in their careers. Those subjects reported feeling *less satisfied* with their careers. Also, when asked to indicate which personal aspect of themselves they liked least, they were more likely to select "career" (see Figure 4.7).

I would probably feel better if I had a more satisfying career. My job is extremely stressful for numerous reasons (including inconsiderate dictatorial management, long hours, low pay, and few if any benefits). I could go on, but you probably get the picture. I am working full time and am barely able to meet my financial obligations. There are no extras such as vacation

Figure 4.7
Percent of Subjects Who Reported Liking Their Careers Least About Themselves from a List of Personal Attributes

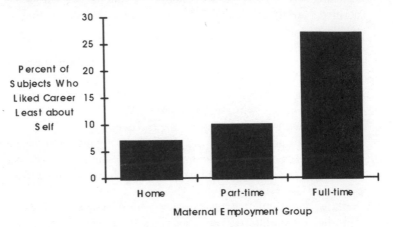

trips; we are doing well to keep the bills paid, food on the table and clothes on the kids' backs. (We don't buy clothes for ourselves except on rare occasions.) I am over-worked and underpaid and it hurts. *(FM2)*

When I worked outside the home, it was in a part-time low-pay position, and done strictly for financial reasons. I did not feel "pride" in the work outside of the home. *(FM2)*

Sadly, even the subjects' husbands seemed dissatisfied with their wives' careers (see Figure 4.8).

A discrepancy between attitude and behavior of daughters of employed mothers was apparent in the literature. As early as age seven, girls with mothers working outside the home recognized that nontraditional careers were open to them; they also felt that they did not want (or would be unable to handle) traditionally masculine careers (Bacon and Lerner, 1975; Marantz and Mansfield, 1977). Bacon and Lerner (1975) hypothesized that the daughters either felt confusion at the large number of careers open to them or were aware of the social difficulties for women in nontraditional careers. A third response, besides those indicated by Bacon and Lerner, might be

Figure 4.8
Proportion of Husbands Who Were Perceived by Their Wives as Being Dissatisfied with Their Wives' Employment

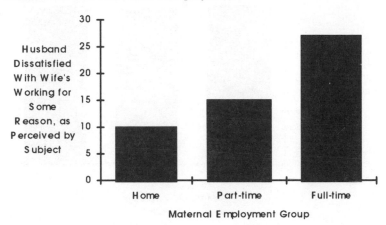

Maternal Employment Group

that the daughters of working mothers perceived they had less control over their lives and their futures.

The daughters of employed mothers, more than the subjects reared by home-mothers, expressed their aspirations to attain more education (Banducci, 1967; Baruch, 1972; Stuckey et al., 1982) (see Figure 4.9). However, the education demographic for the Sugar Study revealed fewer college diplomas among the daughters of full-time working mothers (see Figure 4.10). While 89% of the daughters of home-mothers and 88% of the daughters of full-time employed mothers attended college, 79% of the daughters of home-mothers completed their college degrees; only 57% of the daughters of full-time employed mothers did.

A similar decrease in the percentage of professional careers was evident in the daughters of the full-time maternal employment group. Seventy percent of the daughters of home-mothers considered themselves professional, while 50% of the subjects reared by full-time employed mothers listed themselves as having professional careers. Even though the lack of a college degree may have held back the women in the full-time maternal employment group, the data clearly suggested that both the home-mother and full-time maternal employment groups had equal access to higher education.

The results of this study show that the subjects reared by full-

Figure 4.9
Percent of Subjects Who Had Attended at Least Some College

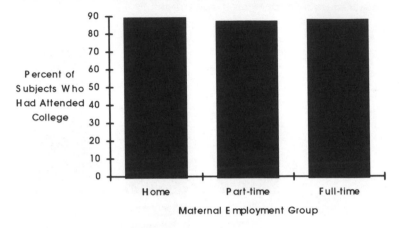

Figure 4.10
Percent of Subjects Who Completed Their College Degree After Starting Higher Education

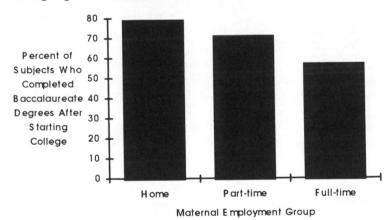

time employed mothers felt less efficacious in their parenting, careers and lives in general. The daughters of full-time employed mothers also felt less satisfied with their lives. The dissatisfaction with careers becomes especially poignant when one realizes the significance of the preference (or need) of the subjects reared by full-time working mothers to be active in careers rather than par-

Figure 4.11
Percent of Subjects Who Were Less Satisfied with Work Inside the Home than Outside the Home

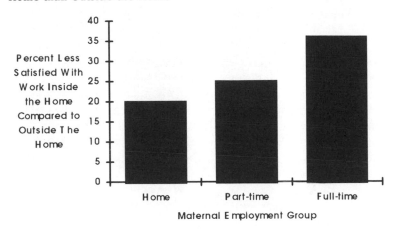

Maternal Employment Group

enting. As a group, they felt even less capable and satisfied in their parenting and homemaking than they did in their careers (in which they also expressed their dissatisfaction) (see Figure 4.11).

How do or did you feel about your work outside the home?

a. More satisfactory than work at home

b. Less satisfactory than work at home

c. About the same

d. Not applicable

From examination of the data, there seems to be little doubt about the negative perceptions regarding parenting skills, career, and life in general of the subjects reared by mothers who had worked full-time for at least nine years of their childhood. Questions have been raised to me whether (1) this particular group of subjects reared by full-time employed mothers was simply aberrant or (2) they were, as a group, unusually embittered by their lives and deliberately trying to "stack the deck" for the study.

Both questions point to valid concerns. In any research that accepts volunteers, the results will often depend upon *who* decides to volunteer. That is one of the major reasons demographic questions are asked of the subjects. In the Sugar Study, the three maternal employment groups did not differ materially on any of the demographic variables except one (discussed in Chapter 7). Remember the pattern (noted so often) that revealed that the test scores of subjects reared by part-time employed mothers fell between the home-mothers' and full-time employed mothers' groups. It lends strong support for the maternal employment influence upon the feelings of efficacy and satisfaction of the subjects. Failing to accept that rationale, we must then ask ourselves, Which group was aberrant? Perhaps the home-mother group was unusually optimistic, efficacious, and satisfied. If that is the case, most of us could probably benefit from some of their "deviance."

The second issue raised concerned the deliberate sabotage of the study by a group of particularly disgruntled subjects; this possibility is considered to be a confounding influence. When the Sugar Study was planned, the possibility that subjects might have felt tempted to champion one life-style over another was taken into consideration. That was the very reason the subjects were not informed that it was *their mothers'* employment and not their own that was the deciding factor in the study. In this way, the volunteers for the study were more likely to answer the study questions without biasing the findings since they did not know the purpose of the study. Chances are still good that a few subjects realized the true goal, however, the likelihood that those few could sway the net results is small.

The knowledge that full-time maternal employment is potentially harmful to daughters may be painful to read. Some might suggest that even asking the question is blasphemous. Perhaps so, but not asking the question risks generations of daughters to come.

As parents we are not actually "rearing children." We are rearing adults. The results of the study suggest that the efforts we make during the first eighteen years of our children's lives will have an effect on them for decades.

5

Depression

Once the excitement of having a new baby in the house wears off, parents are often caught unprepared as reality sets in. If the infant is the first child, Mom and Dad will hardly believe how much of their world now revolves around waking, eating, and diapering. Subsequent children make just as large an impact (although it is not as much of a surprise). Most of all, new parents learn to live with a totally self-centered creature who couldn't care less whether Mom or Dad eat, sleep, have fun, or even go to the bathroom.

I can remember the lowest ebb of my own new parenthood. With two infants under the age of two, the limit of my endurance was reached. I had barely slept for weeks. The baby never stopped crying unless held constantly (half the time she cried then, too). When the baby was finally sleeping, her twenty-one-month-old sister expected and needed my attention. There was simply no room for me, or my needs, anywhere in the equation. One day, sitting on the living room couch, I finally joined the girls' chorus of tears. There the three of us sat, until my husband came home from work, gently took the babies, and let me get some sleep (bless him).

TODAY'S MOTHERHOOD

The unrelenting nature of early child care has become even more difficult in the past few decades. When our mothers lived close to our grandmothers, they could easily ask for help or get a respite from the children. The baby boomers tended to move around, though; "Grandmother" could have been thousands of miles away (or busy with her own career). Also, in the late forties and fifties, the tremendous growth of families ensured the existence of neighbors with their own small children. Support was readily available from other young mothers who knew they would need support tomorrow or next week. However, in the seventies and eighties, population growth had declined substantially. Families could afford fewer children and often delayed having them until well established in careers. When children finally arrived, they were frequently placed in other child-care arrangements as the mother returned to the workplace. Women who remained in the home, by choice or necessity, often found themselves in an intellectual and social wasteland. For blocks around, homes emptied in the morning and filled again in the evening with fatigued, overworked parents and cranky children ready only for a supper, a bath, and bed. When researchers discovered that homemakers were more depressed than their working peers, who could possibly have been surprised? Certainly not the unpaid, unsupported, and lonely housewife and mother!

I will probably return to the workforce in a few years to help with income and so I'm not bored! I do know, now, that stay-at-home Moms don't have it so easy—we don't sit around watching soap operas all day, living a life of leisure. I think an awful lot of women who work are really the ones taking the "easy way out" to let someone else "raise" their little ones. (FM2)

It is very hard (& lonely) being an "at-home" mom—all the women on the street work full time, no one to stop in for coffee like when I was growing up! The area children go to day care, so you have to "import" friends. (HM2)

With two young children I feel like I can never get anything accomplished, they are always making demands on me and there is never time to do just what I want to do, which at this point even if I did have the time I no longer know what I'd want to do. (*PM2*)

After I had my child, I knew I had to go back to work because I couldn't stand being home. I needed to get out and be with other people. (*PM2*)

The hard part is the demands on my time from my two young children. Also, being a homemaker can be lonely. (*PM2*)

My work inside the home is boring, repetitive, lonely. I miss the contact you have with adults at work, the conversation, the stimulation of a busy office, deadlines. At home it [is] pretty much the same day after day cooking, washing, cleaning up. It never ends and it's a constant. (*PM2*)

I constantly battle low self-esteem over being a full-time home maker. Even though my spouse agrees with my decision to stay home, even he expresses subtle criticisms. (*PM2*)

Doesn't the working mother get some of our concern, you might ask? Of course she does. Dual-income families keep grueling schedules with virtually no letup.

I am very proud of my work as a teacher and it is very fulfilling. However, I have recently left the field to be home with my children, 3, 7 and one on the way. While I was teaching (1 1/2 yrs.) I didn't feel my family received the proper attention and TIME from me that they so deserve. I was ALWAYS tired. My husband is self-employed and works very long hours. It didn't seem fair to me to have both parents as "frazzled workaholics." I didn't want to see my kids end up like some of the troubled 15 yr. olds in my classes. (*HM47*)

The second year of teaching school after their birth was much more traumatic. The twins were 18 months and had just spent every day with me for 12 weeks of summer break. My son howled every morning, and the sitter said he cried for almost an hour each day. I would sometimes cry all the way to work. (*PM2*)

There's always too much to do and not enough time! Definitely not enough time to just play with my children. It's frustrating and aggravating and sometimes depressing. (*PM2*)

I wish I had had more children. I wish I could stay home in the summer with my son. I always feel pulled by home/work responsibilities and always feel inadequate in both areas. (*PM2*)

Although I enjoyed it—loved the pay check and feelings of self-worth—I sincerely missed my daughter. I was tired a lot, stressed a lot, felt as though I never had enough time in the day or on the weekend. (*PM2*)

I still feel the overall responsibility when I am at home. As a result, I am tired most of the time because I work all day, then go home to another demanding full time job of raising kids and managing a household. (My husband keeps the house clean and kids fed during the day, but I do all the shopping, laundry, finances and the evening meal.) (*PM2*)

A difference in rewards is apparent between employed and nonemployed mothers. Women who work outside the home get constant feedback from other adults who value their contribution. Even if positive comments are few and far between, working women can count on their paychecks, a powerful symbol of their work contribution. This validation of "worth" has far reaching consequences since it provides their families with a higher standard of living and it bolsters the women's sense of competence. In many ways, these factors mitigate the conditions of stress and fatigue noted by mothers in dual-income families.

For the women who remain in the home to care for infants, children, or teenagers, validation of self-worth must come from within. Infants cannot tell their mothers of their appreciation. Children seldom think of thanking their moms.

She was always there. (*HM1*)

I never thought much about it. All the mothers in my neighborhood stayed at home—it was standard. It was good to have her there. (*HM1*)

I took my mother being at home for granted, and, I think, so did she. I'm fairly certain there was never any sense of a choice being made. I don't think my mother valued the worth of what she was doing although she clearly enjoyed it. (*HM1*)

As for teenagers, any mother of a teenager will tell you to look over your shoulder quickly if a teen gives you a compliment. Husbands only seem to notice the housework if it is not done, or not done well enough.

As my daughter has grown I enjoy sharing the world with her and I have more free time but I sometimes feel I don't get the same positive feedback and satisfaction for projects completed that comes from a work environment. (*PM2*)

Caring for a home and children can be an exciting and fulfilling part of life, but the rewards are subtle. More than subtle, the true value of mothering can take years (perhaps decades) to become manifest.

Sometimes I think if I worked I would feel much better about asking for money, etc., but I know I'm doing the job I'm supposed to do by just being home for my children—maybe someday I'll get my reward! (*FM2*)

With so little support from family, friends, and society, only very secure women can maintain optimism about their lives.

[*Author's note*: Believe me, in the middle of a very difficult day, the knowledge that *someday* someone *might* be grateful for the work I've accomplished in the home is cold comfort indeed!]

MATERNAL EMPLOYMENT AND CHILDHOOD DEPRESSION

The relationship between maternal employment and childhood depression has seldom been addressed; some studies have shown no difference in emotions between those children reared by employed women and those raised by mothers who remained in the home. Shaffer and Emerson (1964) found that the intensity of an infant's attachment with the mother is related to the mother's responsiveness and stimulation, not to the amount of time she spends with the infant. In other words, it is the quality rather than the quantity of time with the infant that is important. Moore (1969) discovered that children in stable substitute care were no more disturbed than children who stayed with their mothers. In a recent review of the literature, Hoffman (1989) observed few differences among preschoolers of working and nonworking mothers. Hoffman suggested that factors in the family such as parental attitude, the number of hours the mother worked, social support and the child's gender were more salient criteria for research than maternal employment. In contrast, other scholars have indicated that a reduction in time with the parent can be detrimental to the infant (Bowlby, 1969) and that working mothers were less likely to satisfy the security needs of young children (Hojat, 1990).

Although the tendency for depression was not specifically addressed in maternal employment research, the trend for *detachment* was apparent in much of the literature regarding interpersonal relationships of the daughters of employed mothers. Several researchers studying young infants found insecure-avoidant behavior in which the babies of employed mothers tended to ignore their mothers on the mother's return, in comparison to the infants of home-mothers.

Similarly, adolescent depression was not found to be related to maternal employment; yet clinicians in the field tend to urge greater parent availability and involvement to help prevent depression of teenagers. When teenagers were faced with less parental involvement and an empty home, they often felt lonely and abandoned. Again, the common thread that ran through those studies was detachment. The daughters of full-time employed mothers reported more aloofness from parents and peers than the daughters reared by home-mothers.

I was an only child and had no parent at home in my teen years. I developed a bad weight problem and had an extremely low self-esteem. Due to her working my parents had money, but I rebelled against nice clothes and such because it seemed that was all that was important not me. (*FM1*)

My mother attended school when I was 14. I was upset that she was not home when I came home from school. I felt cheated out of her time and was lonely. I had had her around all of the time before that. However, when I was older (about 17 years) I really became respectful of the fact that she was an educated person who was a very hard worker outside of the home. Around the home she always worked hard and I respected that immensely—her work at home was thorough. (*PM2*)

At first it (outside work) bothered me—made me sad, upset that I had to help more at home and mom was gone sometimes, but then I adjusted and felt fine about it. Inside [mother's work inside the home]—helped me learn about housekeeping. (*PM1*)

She worked 2 1/2 days per week. I sometimes felt abandoned when I got home from school but I was proud of her when I saw her at work. (*PM1*)

I have few childhood memories. There was little bonding or relationship. I was just starting to know my mother when she died at age 42. My mother worked to get us out of the city, provide a Christian education and assure college. I miss her, I thank her for her goals met and her sacrifices. (*PM1*)

It is possible that the adolescent drive for autonomy is less traumatic when it is the adolescent's choice to become independent. The feelings of abandonment some adolescents experience may arise if "autonomy" is imposed upon them by their mother's decision or need to become employed.

RATE OF DEPRESSION AMONG SUBJECT GROUPS

The previous research into the effects of maternal employment found that children of working mothers were more detached from parents and friends than the children of home-mothers; the children experienced feelings of loneliness and abandonment. We assume that the vast majority of parents try to give their children homes where they can grow up feeling secure. The subjects in the Sugar

Figure 5.1
**Percent of Subjects Who Mentioned the Word "Secure" or "Security"
in the Open-Ended Question**

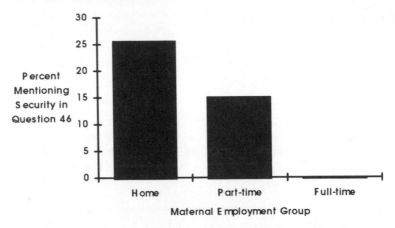

Maternal Employment Group

Study gave a strong indication that, if the mother worked outside the home full-time, the daughter felt less secure. This was highlighted by the revealing responses to the first open-ended survey question, "How did your mother's work inside the home or outside the home affect you?"

Subjects who had been reared by home-mothers frequently mentioned the sense of security they had from their mother's presence in the home (please understand that this response was volunteered by many of the subjects without being specifically requested). In stark contrast, the subjects in the full-time mothers' group failed to mention security even once (see Figure 5.1).

Further circumstantial evidence was forthcoming: Examination of the three maternal employment groups revealed a difference between them in the percentage of subjects who had been treated for depression at some time during their lives (see Figure 5.2).

A two and a half times greater rate of depression for the daughters of full-time employed mothers suggested a serious difference that can be explained, in part, by the perception of reduced levels of self-efficacy noted within the Sugar Study.

I always feel pulled by home/work responsibilities and always feel inadequate in both areas. (*PM2*)

Figure 5.2
Percent of Subjects Who Had Been Treated or Diagnosed as Depressed at Some Time in Their Lives

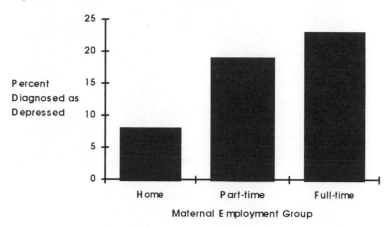

The subjects' loneliness and sadness regarding their childhood seemed to have deepened into depression by adulthood. Theorists acknowledge the contribution the perception of low self-efficacy plays in the development of depression (Bandura, 1982). Higher rates of depression for the subjects whose mothers were in the full-time employed group should not be very surprising: this group apparently missed out on important aspects of psychosocial development because of their mother's employment. Although the subjects in the part-time maternal employment group fared better than or equaled those in the full-time group with respect to the perception of self-efficacy, their means most often fell between the home-mother and full-time employed group. Thus, the doubled rate of diagnosed or treated depression, and greater levels of expressed stress (noted in the next chapter) suggested the subjects reared by part-time employed mothers also experienced a reduced sense of self-efficacy.

When people have a low sense of personal efficacy and no amount of effort by themselves or comparative others produces results, they become apathetic and resigned to a dreary life. The pattern in which people perceive themselves as ineffectual

Figure 5.3
Percent of Subjects Indicating Recent Changes in Their Appetites

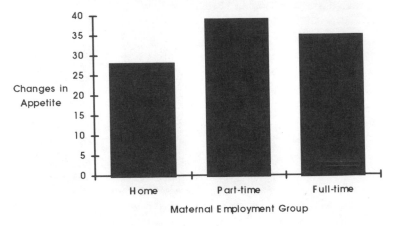

but see similar others enjoying the benefits of successful effort is apt to give rise to self-disparagement and depression. Evident successes of others make it hard to avoid self-criticism. (Bandura, 1982, p. 141)

RATE OF DEPRESSIVE SYMPTOMS AMONG SUBJECT GROUPS

In the Sugar Study, the factor of depression was studied in two ways. The first, mentioned earlier, used the percentage of subjects who had been treated or diagnosed for depression. That factor was a very serious indication of distress (at some time in their lives) for some of the subjects. The second factor sought to determine whether the subjects were currently experiencing any symptoms of depression, which are well known to therapists and psychiatrists. Those symptoms are changes in appetite (i.e., eating more or less than usual), difficulty sleeping at night, and a general feeling of fatigue. Subjects' responses to the eating and sleeping questions did not reveal significant differences among the three groups (see Figures 5.3 and 5.4). However, the subjects in the home-mother group expressed the least symptomatic

Figure 5.4
Severity of Sleep Difficulties Noted by Subjects

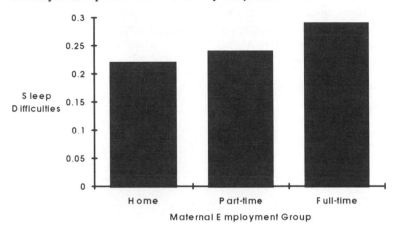

Figure 5.5
Subjects' Perception of Their Level of Overall Fatigue

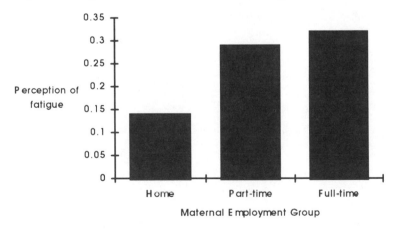

behavior. The question of appetite did not address the possibility of eating disorders.

The third symptom of depression, however, evoked significantly different responses from the three groups (see Figure 5.5). The meaning of the three graphs may be that none of the maternal employment groups was statistically more "depressed" on average than any other group at the time of the study. However, taken as a whole, the adult daughters reared by employed mothers were more at risk for depression and depressive symptoms than the adult daughters reared by mothers who remained in the home.

6

What About the Daughters of Part-Time Employed Mothers?

I became employed part-time to pay for my college costs and a few family extras, while both of my daughters were in school full-time. If I was not home when my daughters were, my husband or their grandmother was there to care for them. It seemed ideal. I could have outside stimulation and financial extras for the family while providing the girls with the "Mom-time" they had grown used to. An example of the flexibility we all enjoyed was an incident that occurred during the writing of this book. My younger daughter needed a dress alteration for the upcoming dance at school. An hour after the request had been made, I was still busily working on Chapter 4 of this book. When I looked up, my fifteen-year-old was standing next to me asking whether the dress was finished yet. Despite the fact that the dance was not for another week, she had wanted to show it off to a friend. We compromised, and the dress was altered during a work break later that evening. My flexible, part-time work schedule enabled me to be available for my daughter.

Part-time employment often has an important role in the lives of mothers. Women can enrich their lives socially, professionally, and financially. They can send the kids off to school in the morning and be home for them when they get off the bus in the afternoon (warm cookies, cold milk, hug and all).For the women who can swing it, part-time employment seems to do it all.

> I feel I am a good role model for my children. Working part time eases the expenses just enough so we can afford little extras (not much though). I love working. But, it makes me appreciate my family more when I'm home. (HM2)

> I currently work on a limited part-time basis—some evenings & weekends when my husband generally stays with the kids. I am comfortable with this—considering myself a "full time mom" right now. (HM2)

> I fluttered between full-time and part-time work. Three years ago I stumbled upon the best of all possible worlds—working third shift. I'm home with the kids, can volunteer at school, and they never had to go to a sitter's. (HM2)

> Part-time work is ideal. I've worked 15–20 hours a week since adopting my son. It's just enough to keep me a happy functioning adult without feeling that I'm cheating my son or husband. My life feels very well-balanced. (HM2)

> Being a full-time mother and part-time employee is the best combination. If it wasn't a financial necessity I wouldn't have worked until my youngest child was 9 or 10 years old. (PM2)

> I was glad to be able to job share and keep my professional job on a part-time basis. I feel I have the best of both worlds by being there to enjoy my 20 month old son and work 20 hours per week. Plus my mom and mother-in-law each baby-sit 1 day a week so I don't worry about baby-sitters. (PM2)

> The time spent working part-time outside the home was the most satisfying. However, after the birth of my second child, I found I wanted to be more available to my family and their needs. The career was put on hold for a few years and I plan to enter the teaching field rather than continue in banking. The schedule would be better for accommodating school-age children. (PM2)

> My husband and I both felt my part time work 15 hr./wk. Sept.–May worked into our family. With everyone O.K. about

my job I can enjoy with little regret the profession I enjoy. (PM2)

I truly love my family and children. I feel that it was very important that I was home with them while they were young. I also feel that since it isn't absolutely necessary I do not want to work full time yet. But I also like the outside stimulation of the workplace. Part-time work seems to work well. I feel like I'm contributing financially and I guess I feel I really have control over my life when I am working. It's quite a paradox. My family definitely comes first and I will always put them first before a job or anything. It's nice that they are getting older too because I can explain to them that Mom needs her own time and they understand and respect me for it. But I would never trade those early years for anything no matter how tough it was. I think it helped me be more compassionate and understanding and it also let my children see how very important a family is—and always will be. (FM2)

MATERNAL EMPLOYMENT AND STRESS

Full-time maternal employment has long been associated with increased stress for the mother. Women who enter the work force are often faced with the prospect of two full-time jobs, one in the home and one in the workplace. The resultant stress on the mother has been found to have negative effects on her children, as increasing global stress leads to a decreasing acceptance of the child.

Many mothers choose to remain in the home until the children are older (teenagers). They may feel that the kids will be able to handle Mom's employment better at that age. Authors have surmised that the increase in family income and the adolescent's need for autonomy help to cushion the problems brought on by the mother's absence and preoccupation with employment. Their theories suggest that the primary developmental task of adolescents is to detach themselves from their parents; in this way, teenagers learn independence and create new alliances that will lead to adult relationships such as marriage. Thus teenagers with working mothers would be nudged into accepting adult independence; they would also be less likely to have an overpowering and doting mother from whom to separate.

> I never felt like my mother really cared for me. My sister was her favorite. I couldn't wait to leave home. They were so strict. Got married too young. Kept making the same mistakes again and again. I was glad when she finally got a job and got out of the house. *(PM1)*

> As I remember, I felt very comfortable with her working outside the home [and] when I grew older I enjoyed the independence it gave me. *(PM1)*

> When I was young, it was, in my opinion, important for my mother to be there especially when I came home from school. As I grew older (pre-teens) I found her being there an intrusion on my privacy. When she went to work I found I enjoyed my freedom but had household duties given to me which I resented. *(PM1)*

> She began working when I began 8th grade. As I think back it really didn't affect me that much—My responsibilities were increased a little—such as making dinner and doing the wash and ironing occasionally. I didn't enjoy her being home when I was younger. *(PM1)*

MATERNAL EMPLOYMENT AND CHILD STRESS

Few studies have looked at the relationship between child stress and maternal employment. In a 1978 Canadian study (Burke and Weir), 181 adolescent girls and 93 adolescent boys thirteen to nineteen years of age participated in a study to determine whether their mothers' employment status had any effect on their sense of well-being. While no significant results were found for the boys in the sample, the daughters of women employed full-time outside the home were significantly more likely to feel they could not approach their mothers or peers with personal problems; these girls also reported significantly greater life stress than the daughters of mothers who stayed in the home. The author stated, "The sources of stress which female adolescents with working mothers found to be most intense suggest that the absence of the mother must leave a substantial void in their lives" and "It seems that maternal employment may be associated with difficulties in the relationship of the parents and this in turn created a stressful environment for the adolescents."

My parents didn't have a very good marriage so my mom spent most of her spare time with me. (PM1)

Mom was a cashier in a drug store—Dad was so jealous he spied on her. She couldn't take it and finally just quit. I hated the arguments and accusations. When Mom cried we all felt bad, when Dad cried we got scared. (PM1)

—caused some tension because my father didn't like my mother working. (PM1)

I remember her always complaining. That made her look like a martyr to me. She would have probably been the same even without a job because my parents never really communicated or shared the same goals. (PM1)

Because of the higher levels of stress and stress-related problems inherent in dual-income families, many mothers have chosen to compromise by working part-time in paid employment. Some research has actually found that a mother's part-time employment was detrimental to her children. Moore (1964) found that children who had mothers with inconsistent work histories were more aggressive and displayed more antisocial behavior. Another study (Collins III, 1975) found adolescents with part-time employed mothers were more stressed and had more personality problems than the children reared by either home-mothers or full-time employed mothers.

INDICATIONS OF STRESS AMONG THE THREE GROUPS

The Sugar Study found similar increases in stress and stress behaviors in adult daughters reared by part-time employed mothers. Nine items addressed stress in the questionnaire. Subjects were asked about their health, legal drug use, use of alcohol, need to seek counseling, worries about their children, and arguments with

Figure 6.1
Level of Reported Alcohol Use Among the Three Groups

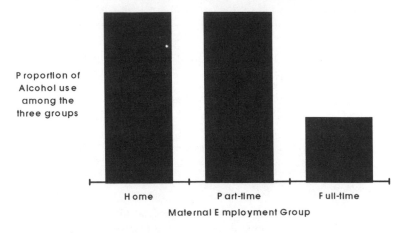

P roportlon of
Alcohol us e
among the
three gro ups

H ome   P art-tlme   F ull-tlme

Maternal E mploymentGroup

husbands. Examination of the three maternal employment groups
revealed that the subjects reared by home-mothers were the least
stressed of the three groups. The Sugar Study finding that daughters
of employed mothers were more stressed than the daughters of
home-mothers paralleled the findings of the study conducted by
Burke and Weir (1978), who found that the adolescent daughters of
employed mothers reported more global stress than the daughters
of home-mothers.

Of the nine items in my study targeting stress, the subjects in
the home-mother group had the lowest level of stress or stress
behavior on six of the items. On two measures, they shared low
scores with the subjects reared by full-time employed mothers. In
only one item did the subjects reared by home-mothers share the
highest rate of stress-related behavior; along with the subjects reared
by part-time employed mothers, they reported more frequent use
of alcohol than the subjects in the full-time employment group (see
Figure 6.1).

Interestingly, the tendency for increased alcohol use mirrored the
findings noted for the adolescent daughters of home-mothers in the
study (Hillman and Sawilowsky, 1991). The presence of mothers in
the home may have prevented experimentation with illicit chemi-
cals, but enhanced a rebellious need to "get away with something."

Figure 6.2
Percent of Subjects Who Had Sought Out and/or Received Counseling

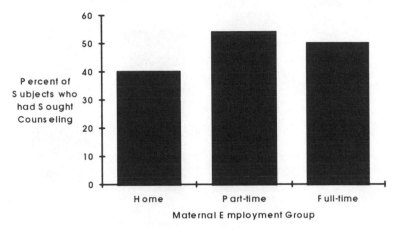

Maternal Employment Group

The case might also be made that mothers who were home-bound, without adequate outlets, indulged in alcohol use in the home more frequently. The daughters may have had greater access to alcohol or may have modeled their mother's drinking behavior.

[*Author's note*: As interesting as the heightened alcohol use by some of the subjects seemed, little can be surmised from their data because the possibility that some of the subjects might have been recovering alcoholics was not addressed.]

The means of two stress-related items were highest for the subjects whose mothers had worked outside the home full-time and part-time. They reported having sought more counseling (see Figure 6.2) and having had more arguments with their husbands (see Figure 6.3) than the subjects reared by home-mothers. Increased arguments with husbands may indicate that the daughters of employed women did not have the opportunity to work out negative relationships with their fathers, as reported by recent researchers (Jensen and Borges, 1986; Mohan, 1990; Paulson et al., 1990). On the other hand, working mothers would have had less time in the home together with the father to provide adequate modeling of marital interactions.

The finding that the daughters reared by employed mothers received counseling more often and had more issues of dissension with

Figure 6.3
Average Number of Issues Noted by Subjects That Caused Dissension in Their Marriage

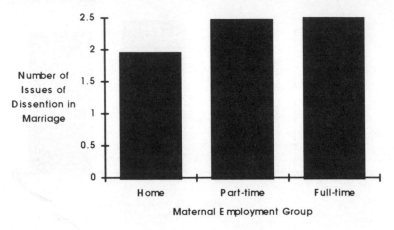

Maternal Employment Group

their husbands than the daughters of home-mothers may be caused by the daughter's lessened self-efficacy, or the perception of lower self-efficacy; they may have felt less able to handle their problems without professional assistance.

The subjects in the part-time maternal employment group displayed the greatest levels of stress on seven of the nine stress items. They reported more worries about their children's behaviors. They also expressed the highest levels of health concerns: the daughters of part-time employed mothers reported poorer health and nearly three times the level of sick days (see Figure 6.4) as the daughters of full-time working mothers (see Figure 6.5).

The subjects reared by part-time employed mothers also reported more use of prescription and over-the-counter medicines than the daughters of full-time employed mothers and home-mothers (see Figure 6.6).

STRESS AND MANIPULATION

The likelihood that half the subjects in the present study (who happen to be the subjects reared by part-time employed mothers) would have so many more health-related concerns, by chance, is

Figure 6.4
Average Level of Subjects' Perception of Health as Determined by the Subjects

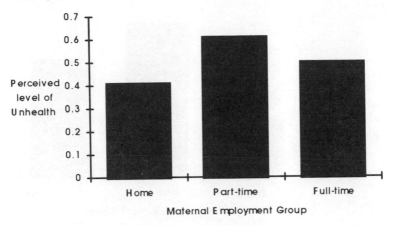

Figure 6.5
Proportion of Sick Days in the Past Year as Indicated by Subject Response

doubtful. In addition, the question arises whether the concerns and behaviors regarding health reflect actual or imaginary ailments. There is a possibility that the greater health concerns indicated by the daughters of mothers who had been employed part-time were hypochrondriacal in nature. This is possible because (1) there are

Figure 6.6
Average Number of Over-the-Counter Medications Used by the Subjects on a Regular Basis

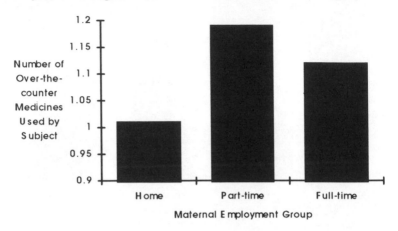

no logical reasons for daughters of part-time employed mothers to have had poorer health and (2) this group of subjects scored the highest in terms of tendency to manipulate significant others in their lives, as discussed next.

The second test administered to the subjects was the Caring Relationship Inventory by E. Shostrum. This test examined the relationship styles of the subjects and their husbands. The subjects were scored on levels of affection, friendship, romantic-love, empathy, self-love, and being-loved scales. In addition, two research scales were examined, deficiency-love and being-love. Finally, two experimental ratios were studied. Here is a description of relationship styles:

1. Affection (A): "agape," a helping, nurturing form of love. It involves unconditional giving and acceptance of the kind that characterize the love of a parent for a child or for a person by God.

2. Friendship (F): a peer love based on appreciation of common interests and respect for each other's equality.

3. Romantic-Love or Eros (E): a possessive, romantic form of

love which includes features such as inquisitiveness, jealousy, and exclusivity.

4. Empathy (M): a charitable, altruistic form of love that feels deeply for the other individual as another unique human being. It involves compassion, appreciation, and tolerance.

5. Self-Love (S): the ability to accept, in the relationship rated, one's weakness as well as to appreciate one's individual, unique sense of personal worth. It includes the acceptance of one's full range of positive and negative feelings toward the person rated.

6. Being-Loved (subscale): the ability to have and accept the other person as he or she is. Being-love includes aspects of loving others for the good seen in them. It is an admiring, respectful love, an end in itself.

7. Deficiency-Love (subscale): the love of another for what he or she can do for the person. Deficiency-love is an exploiting, manipulating love of another as a means to an end.

The scales may be interpreted alone or may be compared to each other. The inventory also includes the Other/Self (O/S) ratio, a ratio between outward loving, expressed toward another person, and inward (self-) loving. As each person in an actualizing relationship concerns himself or herself with their own needs, a proper balance develops from these individually expressed needs. When the balance does not allow for both individuals, a top-dog or under-dog relationship occurs. A second score obtained by combining the deficiency-love (D) and the being-love (B) subscales, the D/B ratio, provides an indication of self-actualization. The lower the score, the more self-actualizing the person is. In contrast, a higher score reflects higher manipulation of others, and lower self-actualizing. The tendency toward manipulation has been noted as one of the major components of hypochondria and other personality disorders (Duckworth and Anderson, 1986; American Psychiatric Association, 1987).

Despite the many significant differences the Sugar Study found among the three maternal employment groups, the three groups did not display *any* significant differences on the scales of the Caring Relationship Inventory. The computed results of the experimental ratios revealed a fascinating difference on the D/B ratio (the deficiency-love/being-love ratio). According to the author of the Caring Relationship Inventory, the high score attained by the subjects in the part-time maternal employment group (higher than those of the two other maternal employment groups and the norm group) indicated a tendency toward manipulation. Higher D/B ratio means less self-actualizing and more manipulation in relationships.

D/B Ratio for Norm Group and Subjects Differentiated by Maternal Employment Group

Home-mothers group	.41
Norm group	.44
Full-time employed group	.47
Part-time employed group	.49

A higher rate of illness behavior has commonly been associated with manipulation (hypochondria) in prominent psychological scales (Duckworth & Anderson, 1986).

Data from the Sugar Study do not indicate clinical diagnoses. At most, the subjects in the part-time maternal employment group may have shown a tendency toward health-related problems and manipulation in comparison with the other two maternal employment groups. The subjects in the study were all functioning well enough in their careers and families to be able to take time out voluntarily for extra activities (i.e., this study). Therefore, an assumption of pathology remains unwarranted for any of the groups.

One reason for the differences noted (for the subjects reared by part-time employed mothers) may be in the nature of part-time employment. The very flexibility sought by the part-time employed mothers may have initiated a pattern of changes intended to adjust to the children's schedule. Sensing they could influence their mother's behavior, the subjects, as children, may have learned to take advantage of her desire to adjust her schedule to fit the child's needs. Because of this, subjects reared by mothers employed part-time may have felt an unreasonable entitlement to have their needs met regardless of their mothers' needs.

My mother worked a short time in an office. I hated it. Rushing out to school in the morning, not home after school. I pretended to be sick a lot and spent those days at Grandma's. I believe it was too much stress for her (home/work, husband and 4 girls) she quit. *(PM1)*

Subjects reared by part-time employed mothers wrote about how their mothers were able to provide extra spending money for their families and at the same time meet every need.

She gave me the inspiration to accomplish my goals—career, marriage, family. I feel she sacrificed a lot in her life for her children, she gave up her career and educational aspirations for us. I never felt neglected. She always made time for me. *(PM1)*

There was more money available for "fun" activities after my mom starting working outside the home. The house work was always delegated to others—everyone helped with all the household chores. *(PM1)*

Mom was always there for me—even when she worked full-time. *(PM1)*

My mother was home every morning to make me breakfast and take me to school and welcomed me home everyday with a loving hug and kiss. *(PM1)*

Comments made by some of the part-time maternal employment group subjects about their adult lives also hinted at a need for special consideration from their husbands and children.

. . . my family has helped tremendously with caring for our home and give me all the support I need. They feel "if mom's happy—everybody is happy!" *(PM2)*

My husband has total control of the kids and household every weekend and I'm in charge Mon. through Fri. I'm tired and my family accepts this and pampers me in small ways showing their consideration. *(PM2)*

My 9 year old son and 6 year old daughter—still crawl up next to me for a hug or snuggling and a day doesn't go by without both telling me they love me. *(PM2)*

Previous studies have noted differences in behavior of the children of part-time employed mothers. The findings of the present study suggest that as the daughters of mothers employed part-time grew up, the patterns of behavior learned in childhood were manifested as stress-related health behaviors in later adult life.

During the months of data analysis I was frequently puzzled by some of the findings. I would ask anyone with the patience to listen whether any of the information made sense; frequently, women would nod and tell me of an incident from their own life that ex-emplified a finding. For instance, one woman (not a subject) told me that she always wondered why she and her father had acted so negatively toward her mother. It seems her mother found a part-time job when the woman was seventeen years old; when both the seventeen-year-old and her father expressed enough displeasure and anger, the mother quit her job. The woman I was talking to then explained that she had been jealous of her mother's new job. The problem, the woman said, was that her mother *enjoyed* the job.

In other conversations, I became convinced that the differences in stress-related behaviors of the daughters of part-time employed mothers might be more than mere coincidence. I told a friend about the increased stress experienced by the children reared by part-time employed mothers. She agreed with the general findings and told me about her daughter, who (in the second grade) suddenly began having stomachaches when my friend began part-time work. After ruling out physical problems, they sought help from the coun-seling profession. The counselor told the mother that the problem was the part-time job. The girl was anxious; she could never re-member whether Mom would be at home waiting for her or whether she would go home to an empty house after school. The mother was told, by the counselor, that staying at home or getting full-time work would be better for the child. In this way, the child would know whether Mom would be at home or not.

Later in the stages of my data analysis, I told the same mother about the finding of manipulation and possible hypochondria among the daughters of part-time employed mothers. My friend reacted quite negatively to this. She responded that her daughter had not been sick and home from school in years. Then, a few seconds later, she got the strangest look on her face and remembered that she had been a home-mother for the last few years.

The finding of stress-related health problems and increased tendency for manipulation may be just an unusual artifact of the particular group of women who volunteered for the Sugar Study. As a mother of two daughters myself, I must admit that my daughters have simply assumed my readiness to alter virtually any and all of my plans for their benefit (see the beginning of this chapter). Perhaps the conscientiousness of the women who choose to work outside the home part-time leads them to overreact to their children's needs and desires?

Any other ideas out there?

7

Mothers and Their Parents

THE PERFECT FAMILY

There is no such thing as a perfect family. Every person on this earth enters adulthood with personal strengths and weaknesses that include the benefits and problems passed on to them by their parents. Be they genetic flaws or results of insufficient parenting, the issues that face us in adult life become our responsibility to correct or accept.

The preceding paragraph appears so obvious to most people that it seems unnecessary to state it. Of course we carry the flaws of our upbringing with us in our lives! It is those imperfections that make us unique and irreplaceable human beings; when we think about the slights and hurts of our childhood, we often assume that no one else can understand how we felt and how those painful events still affect us today. Not only do we bury our problems, in the mistaken idea that no one else has suffered as much, we sadly try to use others' imperfections to excuse our own actions.

In the field of counseling, professional therapists help their clients to better their lives by making healthy decisions rather than the unhealthy choices that required counseling in the first place. To a layperson, the job of the therapist appears easy; why not just tell

clients to stop drinking or stop smoking or stop beating their children? In a logical world, the discovery of unhealthy behavior should
end the drinking, smoking or beating if the client really wanted to
do better. Human beings are far more complex than that. Even
when we sincerely desire to better our lives, old habits and attitudes
conspire to reinforce the familiar behaviors. Professional therapists
are well aware of the tactics used by clients to maintain unhealthy
habits; clients might talk about everything under the sun except
their problems, "forget" to attend scheduled appointments, decide
the therapy is too expensive, or deliberately mislead the therapist
by lying. The term used to group these behaviors together is "resistance." Even when the client desperately desires change, some
small part still wants to cling to the known, comfortable, and secure.
One of the more difficult forms of resistance is the tendency to
assume that one's own problems are not faced by others. Nicknamed
"terminal uniqueness," this form of resistance is frequently observed
by therapists involved in drug and alcohol rehabilitation. Alcohol
abusers are often convinced that no one else can understand their
pain, no problems are as terrible as theirs, no families are more
dysfunctional, and no other spouses can possibly be as unfeeling,
nasty, or clinging as their own. This attitude alone cripples the
therapeutic process (even as it enhances alcohol use) because the
client with such "unique" problems cannot possibly be helped by
merely standard counseling. The consequence of terminal uniqueness is greater distress (even death) as the alcohol abuser maintains
dangerous habits.

To one degree or another, each of us falls for the belief that we
are totally unique. We often assume the pain experienced as children
was not experienced by others and become convinced that our siblings were more favored or immune to parental anger. Perhaps,
deep down, we believed that we deserved the pain and distress. In
this manner, the deficiencies of our parents often seem to be in-
surmountable obstacles to our own adult lives.

> Her work inside the home taught me the need a child has for
> attention, comfort, security, and praise, since I and my sisters
> either experienced these or lacked these at various times. I
> want to provide my children with these elements to a greater
> degree. Also her failure to teach me many homemaking skills

has hindered somewhat my progress toward being a good housekeeper and homemaker. (*HM1*)

Her obsession with cleaning the house or rather ordering her children to clean made me feel more of a servant than a daughter. Which is why I probably rebel against housecleaning as an adult. (*HM1*)

She was (is) obsessed with her house being perfectly clean to the point family members no longer feel comfortable staying there. I likewise have a need for organization but not "sterilization." She had many hobbies and outside interests but tried to convince us that she sacrificed everything for "the children." I liked having her there (at home) every day but feel I am less assertive socially than I would like to be due to my limited participation in outside activities. We did not have a lot of extra money and I tend to overspend on my own children, so they would not feel as I did that everything I got was given grudgingly. None of my friends' mothers worked so I did not really think about it much as a child. She would often make us (6) kids feel guilty about the amount of housework she did, as if to give the impression that if we weren't there she wouldn't have any housework? A lot of resentment, fights in later years. It has been hard for me to accept, as an adult, that I do not have to live by her standards or impose them on my children and I sometimes catch myself using one of her "lines." (*HM1*)

Inside the home mom was meticulous and I can feel like a slob for not being neat myself. Mom spent too much time on chores and made us do the same, thus Sat. was not spent with friends and I resented this. I can't waste time thinking staying home and cleaning or go have fun to this day. (*PM1*)

My mother worked inside the home while I was young. She always took care of us and did too much for us. We are less independent as adults because of that. (*PM1*)

She was always there when needed because she was always home. The one drawback was that I never had to do anything for myself—so it was difficult when I was first married. (*PM1*)

My mother gave everything to the children and my father. I now find myself doing the same thing. I wish at times I could give less and take more, but I usually sit back and wait for someone to notice that I need something. This is my husband's biggest complaint about me. That I just don't take what I want. (*PM1*)

The question we should all be asking ourselves is not whether our parents hurt or hindered us, but how we may better our own attitudes and parenting skills for ourselves and the benefit of our children.

FAMILY RELATIONSHIPS

The family is a very important environment for the formation of life and personal values; individuals who feel good about their families also tend to feel good about themselves. Children learn what to believe and how to behave from their parents and pass that knowledge to the next generation (DeMartini, 1985). Contrary to the popular "generation gap" belief, the younger generation *wants* to pass down the attitudes and life-styles of their elders. Mannheim suggested that different generations "work up the material of their common experience by using rather than rejecting the values of parental generations" (in DeMartini, 1985). These values may be (among others) religious, political, and general life orientation (Whitbeck and Gecas, 1988). Researchers have discovered that dysfunctional family values are also likely to be passed on from one generation to the next. Chaotic family environment, sex abuse, poverty, and drug abuse have been considered to have roots in previous generations. Family violence tends to be higher when one of the spouses was exposed to violence in the past (Kalmuss and Seltzer, 1989). Child and adolescent abuse has been found to be transmitted from one generation to the next (Kantor, Peretz and Zander, 1984; Pelcovitz, 1984). Furthermore, children of divorced parents may be skeptical of marriage and become more likely to fail in their own (Glenn and Kramer, 1987).

Among other factors, the values and expectations passed down from mothers to daughters include the desire to work or not work outside the home; generally, daughters who witness their mothers working are more likely to want to work themselves. Besides the tendency to want outside work, there are unexpected effects of daughters witnessing their mothers' employment.

HOW THE SUBJECTS VIEWED THEIR MOTHERS

As we have seen in the Sugar Study, the subjects reared by full-time working mothers did not feel as happy with themselves or their lives as the daughters reared by home-mothers. In addition, the daughters reared by part-time employed mothers exhibited a mixed pattern of effects, including a perception of lack of choice, greater incidence of depression, and more stress-related behaviors.

Typically, the responses by the subjects to two questions at the end of the survey matched (in tone) the statistical findings of the study. The vast majority of the women reared by home-mothers wrote warmly about their memories of mother and home life while growing up.

My mom was a "homemaker," she was always there, *always*. It gave me a great sense of worth and security to know my mom would be around if my brothers or I needed her. She encouraged us to be ourselves, unique and independent of others, and knowing we had a constant support in her it made it very easy for myself and my brothers to be individuals and pursue interests unique to us and not mainstream. I'm very proud and respectful of my mom. (*HM1*)

She was always there for us and she made being an "at home" mom seem easy . . . house perfect, meals that reflected the proper amounts of the basic 4 and homemade desserts! (*HM1*)

It made me know how important it is for a mother to be at home with her children. I think I would not have liked being sent to Day Care every day. (*HM1*)

Mom stayed at home. It was great. She was always there when I needed her. (*HM1*)

My mother was always there when I needed her. I want the same for my dear children. (*HM1*)

Mom gave me a sense of security by being there for me. I knew she put her children first (after God and husband) and there was never a question of work taking priority. She exposed us to a variety of experiences so later in life when we needed, we felt able to adjust. I have tried already to ensure our oldest (2 1/2 years) is able to experience various activities at her age level. If I was working it would be physically impossible without jeopardizing health, personal outside activities, and family time—much less having a fairly decent attitude! (*HM1*)

This was not always the case, however. Even when the mother remained in the home to care for her children, the mother's problems would sometimes affect the children severely.

My mother devoted her entire working time to home and family. She was more a good caretaker than a "mother," as I perceive a mother to be. Everything she did was for the purpose of impressing others with home and children. She was smothering. She never saw us as individuals, as people. (*HM1*)

She was a frustrated, bored, angry woman. She had an affair *right in front* of my brother and I when we were little. She had/has low self-esteem. I do not value housework. I pay to have it done. I would never live in an angry or fighting relationship. If my husband didn't treat me nicely I would be gone immediately. My mother was physically abusive and my brother and I were both sexually abused by her affair partner while my dad was at work in separate incidents. It only happened once to me. My mother was present when my brother was abused. As an adult, she acts like nothing ever happened, and now that my dad is dead, she wears his wedding ring around her neck and carries his picture (a large one) when she travels. (*HM1*)

QUESTION 1

The comments made by the subjects reared by full-time working mothers gave the impression (in contrast) that they were answering an entirely different question. Instead of writing about the love and security they remembered from their childhood, these subjects tended to write about fear and loneliness. Further, if negative emotions were not being expressed, the memories of these women were more likely to involve the nonemotional events of learning how to be independent, do housework and budget time:

> Show how to budget your time and you can do both things well. (FM1)

> Made me independent and ambitious and not afraid to work outside home. (FM1)

> I felt it was important to stand on my own two feet. (FM1)

As in the other areas of the study, the daughters of part-time working mothers had a mixed picture regarding their lives with their mothers.

> At first it (outside work) bothered me—made me sad, upset that I had to help more at home and mom was gone sometimes, but then I adjusted and felt fine about it. Inside [mother's work inside the home]—? helped me learn about housekeeping. (PM1)

> Enabled me to become independent and self-sufficient. Demonstrated that women can be demanding yet sensitive, and stand up for their rights. (PM1)

> My mother didn't work outside of the home till I was in junior high—and then it was only part time—I realized then that a woman can do both and has the choice. (PM1)

In reading through the subject responses, patterns began to emerge: the word "security" was mentioned often by the daughters of home-mothers, but not at all by the daughters of full-time employed mothers. The daughters of the full-time employed mothers were also far less likely to mention their mothers in their responses. Although explicitly asked to write about how their mothers' work "inside or outside" the home had affected them, almost 30% of the subjects reared by full-time employed mothers did not mention their mothers, or even allude to them (see Figure 7.1).

Figure 7.1
Percent of Subjects Failing to Mention Their Mothers (or Allude to Them) When Requested to Discuss the Impact of Their Mother's Work

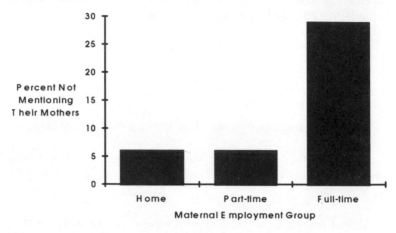

Maternal Employment Group

Could it be that the mothers who had full-time employment during their daughter's childhood were home too little to have sufficient impact? What else could account for such differences in the reports of the subjects?

VIEW THROUGH A PRISM: PARENTAL MENTAL INCAPACITATION

When my advisers, Rita and Fred, and I planned this study, we tried to anticipate situations other than the employment record of the subjects' mothers that might influence the results. One such situation was the possibility that one of the parents of the subjects was mentally incapacitated in some way during the subject's childhood. After all, the presence of mental or emotional problems in one or both parents (as perceived by the subjects) would likely have had profound effects on children; at the very least, it may have confused the issue of maternal employment. With this in mind, the subjects were asked to indicate whether their father or mother had been mentally incapacitated at some time while the subjects were growing up. I gave examples of mental or emotional problems such

Figure 7.2

Averaged Percent of Subjects Who Had Indicated That in Their Opinion at Least One of Their Parents Had Been Mentally Incapacitated at Some Time During the Subject's Childhood

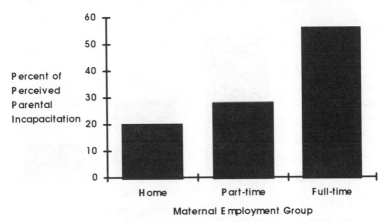

as depression, mania, alcoholism and personality disorders. The plan was to exclude the subjects reared in homes where one of the parents evidenced mental incapacitation at one time or another during the volunteer's childhood. However, results indicated the subjects' interpretation of parental mental health was possibly a factor of maternal employment (see Figure 7.2).

Almost three times the percentage of subjects in the full-time maternal employment group deemed either one or both of their parents to have been mentally incapacitated, in comparison to the subjects in the home-mothers' group. Approximately one-half of the subjects reared by full-time employed mothers believed that one or both of their parents had been mentally incapacitated during their childhood, as contrasted to less than one-fifth of the subjects reared by home-mothers.

The present research was conceived as a study in perception. The subjects reported how they felt about issues regarding their children, husbands, careers, and mothers. The question about their parents' mental health sought the subjects' "opinion" about the mental health of their parents during their childhood; the question of *actual* mental illness remained unanswered. Some of the subjects'

Figure 7.3
**Percent of Subjects Who Stated Their Mothers Had Been Mentally
Incapacitated During the Subject's Childhood When Only One Parent
Was Mentioned**

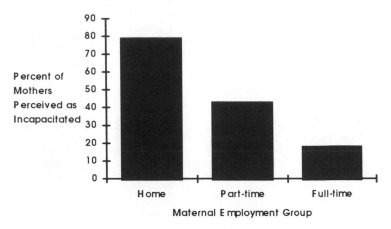

perceptions may have been accurate, while other subjects could
have had faulty impressions accrued as children. The subjects reared
by employed mothers could also have been responding to added
stresses (both the subjects' and their parents') attendant in families
with dual earners. On the other hand, those subjects could have
noted their parents' unhealthy attempts to cope with their stress by
using alcohol or abusive behavior.

MOM OR DAD?

When subjects selected only one parent as mentally or emotionally ill at some time during the subject's childhood, mothers and
fathers were selected at an approximately equal rate. Subjects designated 22 of the mothers as mentally incapacitated (see Figure 7.3);
fathers were designated mentally distressed 24 times (see Figure
7.4). The maternal employment groups differed not only in the
quantity of mental incapacitation reported, but *which* parent appeared mentally incapacitated. Subjects in the home-mother group
chose their mothers more often, and subjects reared by full-time
employed women more frequently chose their fathers as having been

Figure 7.4
Percent of Subjects Who Stated Their Fathers Had Been Mentally Incapacitated at Some Time During the Subject's Childhood When Only One Parent Was Mentioned

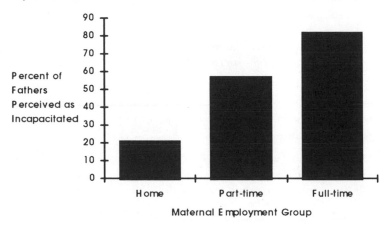

mentally incapacitated during their childhood. The subjects in the part-time maternal employment group had chosen mothers and fathers almost equally.

Even though my mom did not work outside the home she was involved in community activities, church, etc. When my mom stopped all her outside activities, she became depressed and somewhat selfish. (*HM1*)

I felt that this was the way it was supposed to be. I come from a family of 8 children and wasn't really encouraged to higher education. I also remember my mother having what could only be described as nervous breakdowns and as I got older bouts of depression. [A]lthough she was never diagnosed as such. Never sought help. (*HM1*)

She has been diagnosed as manic/depressive and has never sought medical help. She is presently suffering from several medical problems and has the same type of personality as before. (*PM1*)

I feel my mother would have been a better mother had she worked outside the home while her children were small. She seemed highly unfulfilled and sometimes downright strange. I remember as a small child thinking that when my mother was really acting weird, I would fantasize that it really wasn't my mom at all, but space aliens who had taken over her body (!) Things seemed much improved once my mother began working in the school cafeteria 2–3 hours per day. *(PM1)*

My mother is also a high strung woman with phobias about crowds, travel, etc. She is an insecure woman and I don't believe she would have balanced working both inside and outside the home. *(PM1)*

My mom stayed at home until I was 14 years old. She worked one year. She seemed very dissatisfied staying at home and I felt this added to low self-esteem and depression. *(PM1)*

My Dad worked long hours and often two jobs and was an alcoholic (recovered now!) so my mom raised us. *(PM1)*

She worked evenings for several years and there was a lot of verbal abuse from my father because of his alcoholism. He tended to be a lot less abusive if my mother was home. Obviously this caused a lot of problems. However, there's no knowing if it would have been better even if she hadn't worked. *(PM1)*

The unanticipated effects of maternal employment regarding parental mental incapacitation suggested a greater consistency and complexity in the relationships between parents and daughters than had been previously known. Why subjects perceived mental or emotional problems more frequently in one parent or another depending on their mother's employment history remains puzzling. The daughters of home-mothers may have witnessed what appeared to be their mother's struggling with identity in a culture that did not value them as homemakers. The change in the numbers of women working outside the home in the past three decades may have confused both mothers and daughters. The "traditional" or expected role of wife and mother (74% in 1960) became the untraditional role by 1991 as only about 30% of mothers remained in the home to rear their children. The subjects in the present study may have perceived their mothers' choice to stay at home and sacrifice for husband and children as weakness. Even when the home-mother appeared mentally ill to the subject, however, the subject often seemed to accept the incapacitation and still value her mother; for instance consider the following subjects:

> Her lack of respect for herself, set the basis for our relationship, and I never have been able to respect her greatly, or have a warm and close adult relationship with her. I think much of my life was spent rebelling and proving I could achieve much more than her. Ironically, I find myself choosing a lifestyle much similar to hers for my own reasons. I do value the loving, caring example she and my father set for us, both in their own relationship and in how they treated each of their children. I value the security and joy I felt in my own childhood. (*HM1*)

> Despite her problems with alcohol, it was a comfort for me to know she was always there. I want my children to always feel that comfort and security. (*HM1*)

Previous research found the daughters of full-time employed mothers spend more time with their fathers and have poorer relationships with them (see Chapter 2). This factor in turn could have influenced some subjects of the present study to perceive their fathers as mentally or emotionally ill. It may be a case of familiarity that breeds contempt. On the other hand, men with working wives could have suffered greater psychosocial distress, due to their wives' employment and attitudes, that led to emotional ills.

The striking and consistent differences noted among the three maternal employment groups on the rate of maternal and paternal mental incapacitation suggested a linkage between the differences; perhaps a relationship exists. The present study suggested that, as children, the subjects watched their parents closely for signs of mental health. As youths, the subjects may have been predisposed to identify dominant and submissive parents for the purpose of allying with the stronger partner or enhancing selective role modeling. Thus, the daughters reared by home-mothers could have perceived their mother's housekeeping and parenting roles as more submissive and therefore weaker than the father's breadwinnner role that gave the family financial security. Daughters reared by full-time employed mothers might have assessed the father's participation in household and parenting chores (or refusal to participate in essential activities) as submissive or deviant while the mother's financial contribution created a more dominant image.

The rate of perceived mental difficulties the subjects indicated for their parents may seem unreasonably high to many readers. However, remember how you felt about your own parents when you were a young teenager! There are not many of us who can honestly deny that our parents once seemed embarrassingly odd. Didn't Mom dress a little too much like a housewife (or too sexually)? Didn't Dad walk funny, dress like a nerd and smile too much? Other parents were never as strange as your own! Why do you think teenagers are so careful to walk several paces ahead of or behind their parents? Why do they insist on being let out of the family car a block from the school? (Yes, even the family car is woefully inadequate.)

For those of you readers who are parents, I am sure you can remember your children's earliest years. They looked up to you with the awe and reverence that adults reserve for deities. Not only could you do no wrong, but the children actually thought you knew what they were thinking (especially with the x-ray eyes in the back of your head!). How many of us have witnessed our one-year-olds' leap off the coffee table into thin air, as the infants assumed we would always be there to catch them (and we were)? All this lasted until your tiny cherub began to enter the wider world. Then, by observing friends' parents, preschool teachers and extended family members, tendrils of doubt began to emerge. The adoring eyes of your little ones became calculating as they tried to gauge your superpowers next to the preferred abilities of the parents next door. With amazing speed, by the time your children reached the age of twelve or thirteen, your undeniable infallibility was reduced to hopeless bungling (if not downright strangeness).

I have been told that by the age of twenty-one or twenty-two, adult children begin to realize that Mom and Dad are not nearly as odd as they thought. Their parents even become more intelligent! I don't know about that because my girls are still in their teens. However, the individual evolution humans seem to go through, from adoring infant to mortified teen and back again to admiring adult, may be essential to the mature psychological growth of children. If this is so, and if the subjects reared by full-time employed mothers only imagined their parent's incapacitation (as teens may), then why did so many more fail to swing back (in attitude) toward their parents during early adulthood? Could the decrease of time and attention by the mother in childhood have short-circuited the natural sequence of eventual parental acceptance? On a darker note, the subjects reared by full-time employed mothers may, in a way, be denouncing their parents and childhood by labeling them as mentally ill.

On the other hand, if the daughters of employed mothers were accurate in their assessment of their parent's mental incapacitation, we might wonder whether the mental distress was the cause of the maternal employment or the result of it. The daughters of full-time employed mothers may have had a rougher time growing up because of the higher incidence of paternal mental incapacitation; this factor alone may have accounted for the mother's full-time employment outside the home.

In an attempt to find out how the reported incidence of mental incapacitation compared to the reported absence of mental incapacitation among the subjects reared by full-time employed mothers, I separated the subject responses according to whether the subjects had noted parental incapacitation or not. Then I compared each of the two groups independently on the major variables of the study. It turned out that the subjects who indicated parental mental incapacitation felt better about themselves in one-third of the items studied, worse about themselves in one-third and about the same in the final third of the items than the daughters who did not indicate parental mental incapacitation. The net result of this finding is that the subject's impression of parental mental incapacitation had virtually no effect upon the major discoveries of the Sugar Study. The presumed mental incapacitation, either real or imagined (precipitating the mother's employment or caused by the mother's employment), had little to do with the subject's subsequent feelings of efficacy or satisfaction with life.

What all this *seems* to suggest is that:

- Maternal employment is a risk factor which influences the self-esteem of daughters.

- Perceived mental incapacitation suffered by parents is a risk factor that influences the self-esteem of daughters.

- When one or both of the parents were designated as mentally incapacitated by the daughter, the absence of the parents due to employment may have eased some of the problems faced by the child even as maternal employment exacerbated other problems. This may be because the child was physically removed from the ill parent and was therefore permitted to bond with other, healthier adults.

Reflecting back it's probably the best that could have happened. As a result I was raised/cared for by great Grandmo(ther), grandfather ages birth to 7 and with Aunt, Uncle and 2 boy cousins 4 and 10. Paternal relatives who were healthier so it balanced out the abusive behavior. The most difficult years were the ones she was at home with my 2 adopted brothers and she was there when I came home from school. As a result of her working, I was required to be self sufficient and at the time thought nothing about all the chores I had to do. It was only through psy[chology] classes and discussing through college and grad school I learned how different I was, especially because there were only boys in all the extended family. In 1st grade I'd come home to an empty house, prepare the potatoes, salad, veggies, set the table, do my homework, take a bath and turn on the oven for dinner for my parents—my mom got home about six, I'd be home from 3. I did this everyday except for 2 days a week when I waited at home for my mom to go have dinner at my grandparents' (paternal). Consequently, I manage a phenomenal workload of diverse activities that amazes most people and I just thought everybody did it like this. So I guess it has all worked out for the best but I owe a lot to the grandparents and my aunt and uncle who provided the necessary nurturance and positive strokes. (FM1)

8

What Now?

No one in his or her mind could possibly be *happy* with the results of this study. The discovery that over two-thirds of the young women and girls in the United States are at risk for impaired self-confidence, depression, and reduced satisfaction in life is tragic. The high correlation between maternal employment and perceived suffering in daughters was neither expected nor desired. However, only with this knowledge may we begin to make the alterations in life-styles and attitudes necessary to alleviate the pain experienced by women reared by employed mothers and prevent damage to future generations of girls.

The subjects of the Sugar Study were products of relatively ideal situations; they were reared in middle-class or upper-middle class homes by parents who did not divorce. Almost without exception, their fathers were employed throughout their childhood. In their adult lives, the subjects typically had professional or managerial careers; in addition, the majority of the subjects were married at the time of the study. Researchers and laypersons alike will attempt to find other reasons for the stark differences noted for the subjects reared by working mothers, and they cannot be blamed. I would also like to ascribe the results to some factor other than maternal employment; unfortunately the arguments advanced to date just don't hold up.

THE CULTURE IS TO BLAME!

One of the assertions frequently made by professionals regarding the findings of the Sugar Study (and most research into maternal employment) is that our *culture, not maternal employment*, caused the problems. The implication of such a suggestion is that the biases against the working mothers in past decades led to increased tensions and problems for the children. Various theorists insist that women of the current generation are in the midst of social change and that studies regarding maternal employment and its effect upon children are flawed; the culture is in the midst of transformations that make any study obsolete by publication date. However, scholars have expressed the same sentiments for decades. Stolz (1960) cautioned, "Certainly, studies done before World War II were made in a cultural milieu relative to maternal employment which differed considerably from recent years" (p. 773).

The researchers seemed eager to assume that the negative effects of maternal employment on children accrued from the culture's slowness in coming to terms with the increasing proportion of mothers working outside the home. They often maintained that as society came to expect and respect women in the workplace, negative effects of maternal employment would disappear. Wallston (1973) asserted, "Thus, cultural acceptance (of maternal employment) can mitigate guilt, and possibly alleviate some of the negative effects of maternal employment" (p. 93).

By 1983, Montemayor and Clayton wrote: "With more and more mothers entering the labor force, maternal employment is becoming increasingly accepted. This gradual disappearance of the social stigma associated with maternal employment may result in fewer negative effects on adolescents" (p. 116). Then, in 1989, Hoffman addressed the issue of negative effects on children of employed mothers and implicated the cultural milieu itself as the cause: "It is the disequilibrium of social change that creates problems; the typical American family is a dual-wage family, but neither social attitudes nor social policy are in synchrony with this fact" (p. 290).

The results of the present study encourage a reevaluation of the effects maternal employment has on daughters. Perhaps the problems children experience when their mothers work outside the home actually are related to maternal employment. As early as 1920, studies searched for and found a variety of negative and positive effects (some significant and some nonsignificant) of maternal employment on the daughters of employed mothers (see Chapter 2). Yet in a 1989 review of the literature, Hoffman summarized the effect of maternal employment on daughters: "Where differences were found, however, they tended to show positive effects for daughters, whereas for sons the data indicated a mixed picture" (p. 283).

The problem with the issue of cultural change is that the only time cultures don't change is when they are extinct. Each generation has the myopic view that it is the *only* generation to live through such exciting, difficult, and unique times. In a sense, change alone may be the only circumstance differing generations have in common.

Siegal and Haas (1963) suggested that researchers might actually approach the area of maternal employment with preconceptions and biases:

> Early studies of maternal employment, like contemporaneous studies of other social phenomena, often reflected a clear initial bias on the part of the research worker. While some studies have proceeded to damn the working mother, others are examples of special pleading in the attempt to "exonerate" her. It is perhaps not irrelevant to mention that the research literature on working mothers has been created very largely by women scholars (p. 515).

Theorists also seemed to assume that the disapproval by society for working mothers would negatively influence the offspring of employed mothers as well. For children, though, the immediate environment of home and family, and in particular the mother, may be of greater importance than cultural attitudes.

Despite our amazement in watching children as they master complex machines such as computers and the ubiquitous VCR controls, children have changed very little over the last ten thousand years. They start life as helpless, egocentric tyrants and learn to control themselves and their environment through the care and guidance of others. The results of the Sugar Study indicated that (as infants, children, and adolescents) humans require the love and nurturing of at least one constant adult to become self-confident, happy and mature adults. Whether that adult can also be a nurturing father is a question that must still be investigated.

REPLICATE THE STUDY!

Another suggestion given to me is that the study should be performed again in twenty years, to see whether the next generation will also suffer from their mother's employment. I agree that this would be a fascinating task; unfortunately, it will be impossible to replicate this study in twenty years because there will be virtually *no* children reared by mothers with *pure* home-mother backgrounds. Thirty-six percent of the subjects of the present study had been reared by home-mothers for their entire childhood. That percentage made a very respectable proportion, permitting statistical comparisons. However, only 16% of the subjects themselves had been home-mothers for the entire lives of their children and the majority of those subjects were new mothers with infants at home. Now that a full year has passed, some of those mothers have already returned to the labor force (several subjects stated their intention to return to work within the next year). This situation means that the chance that a child will reach the age of eighteen reared by a home-mother for her entire childhood is likely to be 5% or less (see Figure 8.1).

WHERE DOES THAT LEAVE US?

Ultimately, the choices regarding maternal employment must be made on a personal and individual level. No one but the mother has the right to make such an intimate and far-reaching decision. As with other choices, loving parents must weigh the alternatives as well as they are able. Is a life in "poverty" or with insufficient health care more detrimental to the child than the absence of the mother? Should children be exposed to bored and bitter mothers who would be happier working outside the home? Such Solomon-like judgments must be made by all women who choose to become mothers. Unfortunately, there are simply no correct answers that

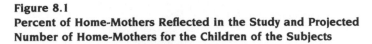

Figure 8.1
Percent of Home-Mothers Reflected in the Study and Projected
Number of Home-Mothers for the Children of the Subjects

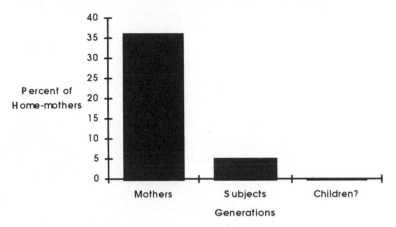

will guarantee a happy outcome for everyone. Hard as we may try, we cannot be perfect parents or provide perfect homes any more than our parents could. As with every other generation, our children must carry the consequences (good and bad) of their parents' decisions.

The subjects who participated in the Sugar Study told us, with their answers and comments, that the presence or absence of their mothers (due to employment choices) had enormous impact upon them for one to almost three decades beyond childhood. That represents a remarkably long-term consequence. Until now, researchers had been unable to find consistent information about daughters of full-time working mothers. You may be wishing heartily that I had not asked the questions and had not found these answers. The findings are not the results I would have chosen to discover. My life would have been much simpler if I had discovered that daughters of employed mothers felt better about themselves (or at least no worse) than daughters reared by home-mothers. After all, the majority of mothers (myself included) work outside the home. Regardless, now that we have more knowledge about the effects of maternal employment, can we ignore it?

WHAT CAN MOTHERS DO?

Fixed answers for the question, "What can mothers do?" do not exist. A simple solution might be that all mothers with children under the age of eighteen should stay home with their kids; this is a black and white solution to a problem with many hues. Every situation is distinct. Every mother is unique and children have differing needs. The suggestions and information in the following sections are based upon logical conclusions of the study. They are recommendations rather than mandates partially because no one has the right to tell you how to lead your life. In addition, because the results of the study are so new and startling, we have little knowledge about possible solutions or their effects. I have little doubt that parents, educators, and social scientists will develop creative solutions to the dilemmas highlighted by the study.

Most of all, no one should permit herself to feel guilty. None of us knew what the effects were. Even with this knowledge, many of us truly have little control over life's circumstances. Finally, there is too much work to do before we can wallow in self-recriminations!

To Home-Mothers

If you are a home-mother, chances are that you feel you have been rearing your children virtually in a vacuum. You are more likely to be depressed than your working peers, and you probably have been considering going to work within the next few years. What do the results of the study mean to you?

Primarily, the results of this study are a validation of your decision to stay at home to rear your children. Remember all the times you felt you had to defend your choice? You watched your working friends go off to work in the morning wearing nice clothing, enjoying expensive vacations, and having so many extras you could not afford. Deep down inside, you knew that children needed their mothers. You had to believe that, because you probably received a lot of subtle criticism from your husband (when he was feeling financially stressed) and not so subtle complaints from your children who wanted to know why they couldn't have the latest toys, games, clothing, or trips that their friends got. Now when your little rag-a-muffin complains about not getting the $200 running shoes, you can just smile serenely at the "underprivileged" kid and say, "Yeah! Isn't it great?"

Do the results of the study mean that you should never get a job outside the home? No. Family or personal circumstances may require your employment some day. As long as you are able to stay home and want to be with your children, stick by your convictions. Don't be swayed by older children or teenagers who try to belittle you because of their own insecurities. How often have our children told us to "Get a life, Mom!"? Always remember, youths are too immature to understand the real world consequences of their mother's return to work. The average teenager will likely think about the larger allowance, better clothes and great vacations when asked whether Mom should get a job. Few, if any, will consider the attendant increase in housekeeping chores, family responsibilities, and loneliness. By the way, the same issues tend to hold true for husbands as well. Your husband probably has a very vague idea of the various roles you fill as a housewife and mother. If your services were suddenly to disappear, he would probably not be happy despite the extra income. As parents and adults, we have a duty to rear our children as we see fit, not as the children, neighbors, friends and media tell us.

Reading for Home-Mothers

What's a Smart Woman Like You Doing at Home? By Linda Burton, Janet Dittmer, and Cheri Loveless. Acropolis Books LTD.: Washington, D.C., 1986.

Staying Home: From Full-Time Professional to Full-Time Parent. By Darcie Sanders and Martha Bullen. Little, Brown and Company: Boston, 1992.

Home by Choice. By Brenda Hunter. Multnomah Press: Portland, Oregon, 1991.

Women and Home-Based Work: The Unspoken Contract. By Kathleen Christensen. Henry Holt and Company: New York, 1988.

To Mothers Who Work Part-Time

The results of this study regarding the findings for daughters of part-time employed mothers have been especially difficult for me

personally. Not only did I believe that my daughters were not hurt
by my part-time jobs, I truly thought that Mary and Robin would
benefit. It seemed so logical that female children would, themselves,
feel more competent and positive if they were able to witness their
mothers performing competently in the outside world. The scores
in the Sugar Study for the daughters reared by part-time employed
mothers were frequently between those of the home-mother and
full-time employed mother subjects. We cannot blithely dismiss
those differences. Even as I sat at the word-processor (at home),
writing the dissertation and this book, my daughters let me know
in words, actions and attitudes that they were jealous of the time
and attention my work took away from them. Even more, they
seemed jealous of the study itself. They also seemed to feel that
they were somehow less important to me because I was *enjoying*
my work.

At first, I wanted to drop all of my professional aspirations. My
vow had been for years that I would stop any job or outside activity
if it was hurting my children. It just never occurred to me that
working the four or five hours a week, outside the home, would
affect the girls at all! Eventually, common sense prevailed. I realized
that my girls were already the daughters of a part-time employed
mother. My quitting a job or career could not change that fact. In
addition, the financial demands upon our family would only increase
as the girls began their own university educations. Not only will I
continue my work, I know I will have to work more to afford their
tuition.

Even if my daughters were much younger or our family were
financially secure, I cannot say that stopping my academic or professional activities would have been an appropriate answer for our
family. How can anyone possibly weigh the voracious and self-in-
volved requirements of children against the very real self-esteem
needs of mothers? Will we finally condense the issue of maternal
employment to a question of who must be sacrificed—child or
mother? I sincerely hope not!

If the effects of part-time maternal employment involve an excess
of mothering through guilt (as suggested in Chapter 6), mothers
may be able to alter their parenting styles to mitigate the effects.
The following recommendations were devised because of the increase in stress, depression, and manipulation style noted for the

subjects reared by part-time employed mothers. Reducing the level of guilt (and therefore reducing the opportunity for the manipulation by children) felt by mothers who are employed part-time as defined in the Introduction may be accomplished in three ways: Women must realistically assess (1) the mother's emotional needs, (2) family financial demands, and (3) child-rearing issues.

The emotional needs of the mother should not be taken lightly. Some women are working only because they think they should and not because they really want to. If that is your situation, you now have permission to quit. You are valuable enough as a mother, without having to prove that you are able to survive in the economic world. However, many women need to stretch their minds in creative pursuits or are contributing financially to their family.

Speaking of finances, the paycheck of a part-time employed mother can sometimes make the difference between having furniture or sitting on the floor in some families. In others, that paycheck may go to purchase health insurance or better food. By understanding the family's financial needs (the definition of "need" will vary from family to family), women can assess the importance of their employment. In situations where the mother has no choice but to work, she should not allow herself to feel guilty. Instead, she could use the information garnered by the Sugar Study to improve her parenting skills.

Child-Rearing Issues

- Whenever possible, the working and nonworking schedule of the mother should be consistent. Regardless of the age of the children, consistency is vital to their sense of security.

- Try never to make a promise to your child that you are unwilling or unable to keep. Whether the promise involves a reward or discipline, your child needs to know that you mean what you say.

- Leave your work at the office. Whether you love your work or hate it, your children need to know that they are more important than anything else in the world to you. In the self-centered world of the child, how you feel about your job is totally insignificant.

- Do not permit your children to make you feel guilty if you are unable to fulfill every whim. Children are very bright; if they sense any weakness in your position, they will take advantage of it to get what they want. What they want is not necessarily what they need or what is good for them.

• Learn to accept the premise that "quality" time with your child is not always pleasant. In the desire to enjoy time with their children, many parents have failed to understand that one of their most important functions is that of disciplinarian. Training children and adolescents to become socially acceptable is not always fun. Being able to discipline children takes time, effort and creativity. Failing to teach children acceptable behavior is easier at the beginning (they are so cute anyway), and much more difficult later as they approach adulthood without the skills they need to be acceptable. Parents *always* pay for their children's behavior (in time, in effort, emotionally, and financially); they either pay early, to teach their young children properly, or they pay dearly during adolescence with an out-of-control teenager.

• Do not let yourself avoid difficult parenting tasks or difficult days by *escaping* to work. The lure of an orderly workplace can overwhelm some parents when chaos breaks out at home. When you avoid painful or unpleasant tasks at home by leaving, your children not only feel abandoned, in a sense they are abandoned (and they know it). Mothers and fathers need to love and stand by their children, warts and all.

• Teenage children still need supervision. They do not need the same care that younger children require, but leaving adolescents to their own devices can lead to premature adult activities unsuitable for children. Perhaps families need to band together to provide a new form of care for the older and younger teens.

The following books provide parenting tips that can help any parent learn to do a better job.

Reading Material for Parents

You Can Say No to Your Teenager. By Shalov, Sollinger, Spotts, Steinbrecher, and Thorpe. Addison-Wesley Publishing Company: Reading, Mass., 1991.

Parent Power! A Common-Sense Approach to Parenting in the '90s and Beyond. By John Rosemond. Andrews and McMeel: Kansas City, Mo., 1981, 1990.
Love and Discipline. By Barbara Brenner. Ballantine Books: New York, 1983.
Get Out of My Life: But First Could You Drive Me and Cheryl to the Mall? By Anthony E. Wolf. The Noonday Press: New York, 1991.

To Mothers Who Work Full-Time

After reading this book, the poignant differences among the three groups may persuade the full-time employed mother to give up her job. Such a precipitous action, however, may not be necessary or even desirable. As stated earlier, there is no one answer to the dilemma of maternal employment. The women who make up the population of working mothers in the United States are as varied as any other group. There are at least two categories of full-time employed mothers who work by choice. Some work because they enjoy their careers. Others are employed because they enjoy having a better lifestyle. These mothers have options in their career choices. If you are considering leaving your job to return home to a new career of home-mother, you have more to consider than simply reduced financial circumstances. The career that involved you for so many years has not been just a place to go. You derived much of your self-esteem from the paycheck, social contacts, and sense of a job well done. By leaving your career, you will leave yourself open to isolation, depression and bitterness. Not only might you suffer from this action, your children might suffer as well. Do *not* leave your job until you have carefully planned for your return to the home!

I recently made the acquaintance of a neighborhood woman who returned to the home after six years of full-time employment. She and her husband had decided that the family did not benefit enough from the second income to justify the difficulties of child care or the unhappiness of the children, who missed their mother. Although this woman had a variety of hobbies and talents to fall back on to fill her time, she had not anticipated the isolation of the modern middle-class neighborhood. She learned that the few mothers at home, with their preschoolers, had very little in common with her because her children were in elementary school. Coupled with the loss of her paycheck, homesickness for former workmates, and reduced financial circumstances, she quickly found herself spiraling into depression and an exacerbation of a previous drinking problem. Happily, this woman was able to center herself and pull out of a potentially disastrous situation.

If you are considering leaving the work force to stay at home with your children, read the Note to Home-Mothers earlier in this chapter. The books listed for home-mothers provide many helpful hints about adjusting to the life of a full-time mother. If, however, you have decided to stay in your career, the next section may be of greater interest.

Many women find themselves in positions where they must work. Whether because of financial or psychological need, the quality of their existence depends upon employment in the outside world. If you fall into this category, the purpose of this text is not to condemn your choices or make you feel even more overwhelmed by your situation. Although it is cruel to tell a mother that she is (possibly) hurting someone she loves when she has no alternative, ignorance regarding the potential consequences of our actions benefits no one. To begin with, not *all* of the subjects reared by full-time working mothers were dissatisfied with their lives. The graphs and scores were based on averages and percentages. This means that some of the subjects felt just fine about themselves, their parenting, and their careers. Second, the scores noted in the Sugar Study were a representation of the subjects' *feelings* about their abilities and attitudes. Those scores did not necessarily reflect actual performance deficits. Finally, even if you must remain employed full-time during your children's youth, there are actions you can take to improve their chances of growing up self-confident and happy.

Although the Notes to Home-Mothers and Part-Time Employed Mothers include commonsense suggestions, I cannot give the same to the women who are employed full-time. This is because I have never experienced full-time employment while rearing my children. Nor was I the child of a mother who worked outside the home. The authors of the following books may have the expertise we need to find out what can be done to ease the difficulties of mothers who must work away from their children on a full-time basis.

Reading Material for Full-Time Employed Mothers

The Woman Who Works: The Parent Who Cares. By Sirgay Sanger, M.D., and John Kelly. Little, Brown and Company: Boston, 1987.
Tips for Working Parents: Creative Solutions to Everyday Problems. By Kathleen McBride. Storey Publishing: Pownal, VT, 1989.
The Working Mother's Guilt Guide: Whatever You're Doing, It Isn't Enough. By Mary Hickey and Sandra Salmans. Penguin Books: New York, 1992.
Wait a Minute, You Can Have It All. By Shirley Sloan Fader. Tarcher/Putnam: New York, 1993.
Juggling. By Faye J. Crosby. The Free Press: New York, 1991.
Balancing Acts!: Juggling Love, Work, Family & Recreation. By Susan Strautberg and Marcia Worthing. Master Media Limited: New York, 1992.
The Handbook for Latchkey Children and Their Parents. By Lynette Long and Thomas Long. Arbor House: New York, 1983.
The Superwoman Syndrome. By Marjorie Hansen Shaevitz. Werner Books: New York, 1984.
Reinventing Home: Six Working Women Look at Their Home Lives. By Laurie Abraham, M. B. Danielson, Nancy Eberle, Laura Green, Janice Rosenberg, and Carol Stoner. Plume Book/Penguin Group: New York, 1991.
The Working Parent Dilemma: How to Balance the Responsibilities of Children and Careers. By Earl Grollman and Gerri Sweder. Beacon Press: Boston, 1986.

WHAT IS LEFT TO DO?

For every question the Sugar Study was able to answer (or at least provide information about) several more queries arose. What happened to the daughters who lived in single-parent homes? What is the effect of the mother's employment when that employment is required because of the father's death? Do daughters fare better if the mother loves her work, or hates her work? What happens to families in which the mothers had worked full-time outside the home for two generations, or three? What if the father was a home-father while the mother worked? Are boys affected in similar ways? Finally, what will be the effect for the hundreds of thousands of children who attend(ed) day care centers as infants and preschoolers? This last item is especially worrisome to the author of this study because few of the subjects' mothers in the Sugar Study worked outside the home when the subject was younger than six; there was no indication that *any* of the subjects attended a daycare center (they were primarily in the care of relatives and neighbors). Although many day care centers are excellent, the sheer lack of long-term research is frightening.

Perhaps the most valuable information to be gleaned from the Sugar Study is that the age of the daughter while her mother was employed did not matter. When most of us thought about the plight of the children of working mothers, we usually considered the infants being reared in day care centers or young elementary age children returning to empty houses with keys worn about their necks. However, the subjects in this study scored similarly to each other (in their respective groups) regardless of when their mothers had employment. We frequently presume adulthood for older teenage children because they look like adults and may speak like adults. But the self-confidence, self-control and self-sacrifice essential to the development of mature citizens are more than superficial markers of adulthood; they are hard won experiential attributes that mere intelligence and creativity are unable to produce.

As members of the earth's animal kingdom, humans are (we presume) the most intellectually evolved; we also require the most time and effort for the rearing of our young. Unlike many animals that can fend for themselves shortly after birth, human infants require nurturing for decades. They also need extensive education to survive in their complex social environment. With every technological advance, our world and our culture become increasingly complicated. Concomitantly, the more complex the environment becomes, the more nurture and discipline (teaching) our children will need.

When I started my graduate school career, the idea of coming up with an original concept for the dissertation (or any research) was daunting. It seemed that everything worth doing had already been done. Now I know that despite tens of thousands of journal volumes, we still have a very tenuous grasp upon the mysteries of our existence. Regardless of the budget crunch facing our nation and academia, there is no option except to proceed swiftly to answer the questions posed here and many others.

We all live within larger contexts of community and nation; should these social institutions carry some responsibility for the difficult situations mothers find themselves in? How can they not? When we walk through a mall that provides no benches for the shoppers, the unspoken message is to keep moving, keep buying, or go home. Neighborhoods that have no sidewalks tell us implicitly that each home is an isolated unit and friendship between neighbors is not a priority or even a consideration. In much the same way, our society (culture, government, economics, etc.) has pushed mothers toward the workplace. It does this by not providing national health care, by instigating economic depression and inflation through fiscal and resource mismanagement, by increasing taxes, and by telling mothers they are not important unless they work. Finally, after putting families into economic double-binds, our culture has failed to provide for adequate child care, catastrophic leave, sick child care, or relief in the home.

Can the message sent by our government suggest anything but the denigration of children's needs and a fostering of the assumption that women (and men) are replaceable cogs in the economic machinery? The short-term advantage our government seems to enjoy—two parents to pay taxes and buy more consumer goods (more taxes again!)—is just that, short term. Our society is unwittingly undermining the self-esteem and mental health of our youth; to keep a questionable economic strategy afloat, our social system is cheating the adults of tomorrow. We have known for years that the generations following the baby boomers will have to foot the bill for the national debt, live with reduced expectations, and support the largest number of elderly poor in history. Now we face the fact that the next generation may also be paying the ultimate price of their parent's employment decisions with their very selfhood.

We can never again let our culture regress to the point where it arrogantly sacrifices women for the sake of the children (or men or the economy). Instead, we must create a society that will permit women to sacrifice for their children if they choose to do so. Only then will freedom and equality have any meaning for humankind.

Appendix: A Statistical Analysis

In this doctoral dissertation study, the experimental design, instruments, and statistical analyses were all under the rigid supervision of my advisers, Rita Myers and Fred Wallbrown. However, I recognize that such controversial results almost compel even more rigorous examination. Therefore, let me tell you about the survey questionnaire and the procedures used in the study to analyze the subject responses.

The primary instrument (The Myers-Carter-Sugar Questionnaire) used in the Sugar Study was first developed by Myers (1989) and revised by Carter (1991) for studies of healthy, older, traditional women. The survey addressed issues of demography, satisfaction and stress. For purpose of the present study, items in the questionnaire were adjusted to reflect the younger subject pool, and new questions concerning efficacy and depression were included.

As soon as the first thirty or forty responses had been received and cursorily examined, I immediately realized that the three groups differed on many if not most of the factors in the study. With that knowledge came the understanding that future scrutiny would require impeccable handling of the data. Fortunately, Kent State University provides extensive statistical assistance to doctoral students working on dissertations. So, after placing identifying numbers on the 253 sets of questionnaires, they were turned in to the university research bureau. There, professional key punch operators entered the data into the computer (The raw data were entered twice to reduce error!). Then, my husband, Bob, and I checked every data entry (69,828 data points) against the hard copy of the subject responses. I even created a "viewfinder" to help us do a better job. We found a 10% error rate that was then corrected. Bob and I repeated this procedure, until I felt satisfied with the veracity of the computer printout (we repeated it three times and my husband still speaks to me). Finally, we were able to proceed with the statistical analyses.

A variety of statistical methods are available to researchers. Each formula depends upon the qualities of the data under investigation. In the case of my study, we used the most rigorous tests to ensure a lesser chance of type I error. Type I error is the mistake of assuming that two groups are significantly different from one another when they really aren't. To that end, the multiple analysis of variance (MANOVA) was selected rather than several analyses of variance (ANOVA) in the examination of the efficacy, depression, and stress variables. An ANOVA is a statistical test to determine how much groups are different from one another while a MANOVA is a combination of several statistical analyses, of factors with similar content, to determine how much groups differ from one another. Because my three study groups did not contain an equal number of subjects, I employed the Pillais Trace test of statistical significance (again rigorous) to find out whether the three groups differed significantly within the MANOVAs despite the unequal number of subjects in each group. Finally, on the question items that had produced the significant MANOVAs, a Scheffé test was performed to determine which group or groups differed from one another (the Scheffé test of significance is often used to measure for vague or nebulous theoretical concepts, such as efficacy, satisfaction or stress. It is a conservative test.

Some of the study questions called for different statistical analyses; for example, the question regarding parental mental incapacitation was handled with an ANOVA followed by a chi-square analysis. A chi-square analysis of variance is a test to find out whether the expected occurrence of some factor (such as the perception of parental mental incapacitation) is significantly different from one group or condition to another. Other items needed only a means analysis or percentage calculation. The volume and complexity of most of the analyses required the use of KSU computer facilities. Hand calculations would have taken the rest of my life. An attempt was made in every stage of analysis to reduce the chance of experimenter bias contaminating the data. Although I can never say with 100% certainty that none of my biases was passed on in some way, I can say with all honesty that I tried very hard to maintain strict controls with the goal of preventing contamination.

Although the nature of this book precludes the necessity to parade every statistical finding, the reader may find a simple representation helpful. The following is a scholarly evaluation of one variable in one hypothesis.

This information is also available (along with the other findings) in my dissertation "The Effects of Maternal Employment upon Adult Daughters: A Study of Parenting and Employment Among Women" by Martha Hahn Sugar (1993), publication #9320734, available through University Microfilm International, 300 North Zeeb Road, Ann Arbor, Michigan 48106–1346.

HYPOTHESIS 1.a.

Women raised in families where the mother worked outside the home either part-time or full-time do not differ significantly, in their reported feelings of general self-efficacy, from women whose mothers worked inside the home.

QUESTIONNAIRE ITEM

34. *What has been your overall attitude this last year?*

a. optimistic

b. neutral

c. pessimistic

Table A.1

Summary of MANOVA Procedure for General Efficacy of Subjects Differentiated by Maternal Employment Group

Effect	Statistical test	Value	F-value	df	p<
Maternal Employment	Pillais trace	.11	3.55	8,458	.001

STATISTICAL RESULTS

The result, shown in Table A.1, of the MANOVA for general efficacy indicates an obtained value for the Pillais trace was .11, which translated into an F-value of 3.55 ($df = 8,458$), which is significant at the .001 level.

This result indicated the three maternal employment groups differed on at least one of the items regarding general efficacy. Post hoc univariate F-tests (Table A.2) were performed to find out which of the dependent variables contributed to the overall significance. Three of the four items in the general efficacy variable achieved significance. The results indicated that at least two of the maternal employment groups differed significantly on at least one of the general efficacy items.

The Scheffé procedure was used for the (highlighted) significant general efficacy item to determine which means significantly differed from each other. The result of this analysis is contained in Table A.3.

Subjects selected their general mood of the past year as being

Table A.2

Summary of Univariate F-Tests for General Efficacy of Subjects Differentiated by Maternal Employment Group

Variable	SS	SS Error	df	MS	MS Error	F-ratio	p<
Can finish work	.14	206.50	2,231	.07	.89	.08	ns
Pessimism	*8.11*	*116.17*	*2,231*	*4.05*	*.50*	*8.06*	*.001*
Adequacy	10.41	245.65	2,231	5.20	1.06	4.89	.008
Choice to work	1.60	36.54	2,231	.80	.15	5.06	.007

Table A.3
Scheffé Multiple Comparisons for Pessimism of Subjects
Differentiated by Maternal Employment Group

	Home-mother M=0.36 SD=.59	Part-time employed M=0.52 SD=.73	Full-time employed M=0.96 SD=.87
Home-mother M=0.36 SD=.59			
Part-time employed M=0.52 SD=.73			
Full-time employed M=0.96 SD=.87	*	*	

* Result of Scheffé test indicated the mean of the full-time employed group differed significantly from the means of the part-time employed group and the home-mother group.

optimistic, neutral, or pessimistic. As shown in Table A.3, the daughters of full-time working mothers reported more pessimism and neutral feelings than either the daughters of home-mothers or the daughters of part-time working mothers. For this item, the daughters of home-mothers and the daughters of part-time working mothers did not significantly differ from one another in the level of optimism or pessimism over the past year.

Bibliography

Abraham, L., Danielson, M. B., Eberle, N., Green, L., Rosenberg, J., and Stoner, C. (1991). *Reinventing Home: Six Working Women Look at Their Home Lives.* Plume Book/Penguin Group: New York.

Aburdene, P. and Naisbitt, J. (1992). *Megatrends for Women.* Villard Books: New York.

American Psychiatric Association. (1987). *Diagnostic and Statistical Manual of Mental Disorders.* 3rd Ed. Revised. Washington, DC: American Psychiatric Association.

Amstey, F. and Whitbourne, S. (1988). Work and motherhood: Transition to parenthood and women's employment. *The Journal of Genetic Psychology, 149* (1), 111–118.

Bacon, C. and Lerner, R. M. (1975). Effects of maternal employment status on the development of vocational-role perception in females. *The Journal of Genetic Psychology, 126,* 187–193.

Banducci, R. (1967). The effect of mother's employment on the achievement, aspirations, and expectations of the child. *Personnel and Guidance Journal, 46,* 263–267.

Bandura, A. (1991). Self-efficacy, impact of self-beliefs on adolescent life paths. In *Encyclopedia of Adolescence.* Eds. Lerner, Petersen and Brooks-Gunn. Garland Publishing Inc.: New York and London.

Bandura, A. (1982). Self efficacy mechanisms in human agency. *American Psychologist, 37,* 122–147.

Baruch, G. K. (1972). Maternal influences upon college women's attitudes toward women and work. *Developmental Psychology, 6,* 32–37.

Bee, H. (Ed.) (1978). *Social Issues in Developmental Psychology.* 2d Ed. Harper & Row, Publishers: New York.

Bowlby, John (1969). Attachment. Volume 1 of *Attachment and Loss.* Basic Books: New York.

Brenner, Barbara (1983). *Love and Discipline.* Ballantine Books: New York.

Burke, R. J. and Weir, T. (1978). Maternal employment status, social support and adolescents' well being. *Psychological Reports, 42,* 1159–1170.

Burton, L., Dittmer, J. and Loveless, C. (1986). *What's a Smart Woman Like You Doing at Home?* Acropolis Books LTD.: Washington, D.C.

Carter, J. (1991). Traditional Women: Levels of actualizing in the second half of life. Unpublished doctoral dissertation, Kent State University, Kent, Ohio. (OCoLC)26378300.

Christensen, Kathleen (1988). *Women and Home-Based Work: The Unspoken Contract.* Henry Holt and Company: New York.

Collins III, S. W. (1975). The effects of maternal employment upon adolescent personality adjustment. *Graduate Research in Education and Related Disciplines, 8,* 1, 5–44.

Crosby, Faye (1991). *Juggling.* The Free Press: New York.

DeMartini, Joseph (1985). Change agents and generational relationships: A reevaluation of Mannheim's problem of generations. *Social Forces, 64,* 1 pp. 1–15.

Duckworth, J. C. and Anderson, W. P. (1986). *MMPI interpretation manual for counselors and clinicians.* 3rd Ed. Accelerated Development Inc.: Indiana.

Fader, S. S. (1993). *Wait a Minute, You Can Have It All.* Tarcher/Putnam: New York.

Farley, J. (1969). Maternal employment and child behavior. *Cornell Journal of Social Relations, 3,* 58–71.

Gallup, Jr., G. and Newport, F. (1991, September). Working mothers. *The Gallup Poll Monthly,* p. 22.

Gecas, Victor (1971). Parental behavior and dimensions of adolescent self-evaluation. *Sociometry, 34,* 4, pp. 466–482.

Gecas, Viktor and Schwalbe, Michael (1986). Parental behavior and adolescent self-esteem. *Journal of Marriage and the Family, 48,* 1, pp. 37–46.

Glenn, N. D. and Kramer, K. B. (1987). The marriages and divorces of the children of divorce. *Journal of Marriage and the Family, 49,* 811–825.

Grollman, Earl and Sweder, Gerri (1986). *The Working Parent Dilemma:*

How to Balance the Responsibilities of Children and Careers. Beacon Press: Boston.

Hickey, M. and Salmans, S. (1992). *The Working Mother's Guilt Guide: Whatever You're Doing, It Isn't Enough.* Penguin Books: New York.

Hillman, S. B. and Sawilowsky, S. S. (1991). Maternal employment and early adolescent substance use. *Adolescence, 26,* 104, 829–837.

Hoffman, L. W. (1989, February). Effects of maternal employment in the two-parent family. *American Psychologist,* pp. 282–292.

Hoffman, L. W. and Nye, F. I. (1974). *Working Mothers.* Jossey-Bass Publishers: San Francisco, Calif.

Hojat, M. (1990). Can affectional ties be purchased? Comments on working mothers and their families. *Journal of Social Behavior and Personality, 5(6),* 493–502.

Hughes, G. S. (1925). *Mothers in Industry.* New Republic: New York.

Hugick, L. and Leonard, J. (1990, June). Ideal family situation: Should both parents work? *The Gallup Poll Monthly,* p. 22.

Hunter, Brenda (1991). *Home by Choice.* Multnomah Press: Portland, Ore.

Jensen, L. and Borges, M. (1986). The effect of maternal employment on adolescent daughters. *Adolescence, 21,* 659–666.

Kalmuss, D. and Seltzer, J. (1989). A framework for studying family socialization over the life cycle. *Journal of Family Issues, 10,* 3, 339–358.

Kantor, D., Peretz, A., and Zander, R. (1989). The cycle of poverty: Where to begin? *Family Therapy Collections, 9,* 59–73.

Long, L. and Long, T. (1983). *The Handbook for Latchkey Children and Their Parents.* Arbor House: New York.

Marantz, S. A. and Mansfield, A. F. (1977). Maternal employment and the development of sex-role stereotyping in five-to-eleven-year-old girls. *Child Development, 48,* 668–673.

McBride, Kathleen (1989). *Tips for Working Parents: Creative Solutions to Everyday Problems.* Storey Publishing: Pownal, VT.

Mead, Margaret (1960). *Good Housekeeping.*

Mohan, P. J. (1990). The effect of maternal employment on Mormon and Non-Mormon adolescents. *Adolescence, 25,* 831–837.

Montemayor, R. and Clayton, M. D. (1983). Maternal employment and adolescent development. *Theory into Practice, 22,* 112–118.

Moore, T. W. (1964). Children of full-time and part-time mothers. *International Journal of Social Psychiatry,* Special Congress Issue, 2, 1–10.

Myers, R. W. (1989). [Traditional wives]. Unpublished questionnaire.

Naisbitt, J. (1990). *Megatrends for Women.* Warner Books: New York.

Overstreet, H. and Overstreet, B. (1960). Love is their reason. *Good Housekeeping,* May, 73, 178, 180, 182, 183.

Paulson, S. E., Koman III, J. J. and Hill, J. P. (1990). Maternal employment and parent-child relations in families of seventh graders. *Journal of Early Adolescence, 10,* 3, 279–295.

Peterson, C. D., Baucom, D. H., Elliott, M. J. and Farr, P. A. (1989). The relationship between sex role identity and marital adjustment. *Sex Roles, 21,* 775–787.

Rollins, J. and White, P. N. (1982). The relationship between mothers' and daughters' sex-role attitudes and self concepts in three types of family environments. *Sex Roles, 8,* 1141–1155.

Rosemond, John (1981, 1990). *Parent Power! A Common-Sense Approach to Parenting in the '90s and Beyond.* Andrews and McMeel: Kansas City, Mo.

Sanders, Darcie and Bullen, Martha (1992). *Staying Home: From Full-Time Professional to Full-Time Parent.* Little, Brown and Company: Boston.

Sanger, S. and Kelly, J. (1987). *The Woman Who Works: The Parent Who Cares.* Little, Brown and Company: Boston.

Shaevitz, M. H. (1984). *The Superwoman Syndrome.* Werner Books.

Shaffer, H. R. and Emerson, P. E. (1964). The Development of social attachments in infancy. *Monographs of the Society for Research in Child Development, 29,* 3, Serial No. 94.

Shalov, Sollinger, Spotts, Steinbrecher, and Thorpe (1991). *You Can Say No to Your Teenager.* Addison-Wesley Publishing Company: Reading, Mass.

Shostrum, E. L. (1967). *Man, the Manipulator.* Abingdon Press: New York.

Shostrum, E. L. (1975). *Caring Relationship Inventory: EdITS Manual.* EdITS: San Diego, Calif.

Siegal, A. E. and Haas, M. R. (1963). The working mother: A review of research. *Child Development, 34,* 513–542.

Stolz, L. M. (1960). Effects of maternal employment on children: Evidence from research. *Child Development, 31,* 749–782.

Strautberg, S. and Worthing, M. (1992). *Balancing Acts!: Juggling Love, Work, Family & Recreation.* Master Media Limited: New York.

Stuckey, M. R., McGhee, P. E. and Bell, N. J. (1982). Parent-child interaction: The influence of maternal employment. *Developmental Psychology, 18,* 635–644.

U.S. Bureau of the Census. (1993). *Statistical Abstract of the United States: 1993.* 113th Ed. Washington, D.C.

Wallston, B. (1973). The effects of maternal employment on children. *Journal of Child Psychology and Psychiatry, 14,* 81–95.

Weiner, L. Y. (1985). *From Working Girl to Working Mothers.* The University of North Carolina: Chapel Hill, N.C.

Whitbeck, L. B. and Gecas, V. (1988). Value attributions and value trans-
    mission between parent and child. *Journal of Marriage and the
    Family, 50*, pp. 829–840.
Wilson, J. (1991). The relationship between maternal role modeling and
    gender identity, marital satisfaction and role conflict for dual career
    women with children. Unpublished doctoral dissertation, Kent State
    University, Kent, Ohio. (OCoL)25663270.
Wolf, A. E. (1991). *Get Out of My Life: But First Could You Drive Me
    and Cheryl to the Mall?* The Noonday Press: New York.

Index

About the Author

MARTHA HAHN SUGAR is performing child and family psycho-
therapy under supervision at Human Development and Counseling
Associates Inc., in North Canton, Ohio. She has a Ph.D. in Counselor Education from Kent State University.